CHRISTOPHER RICH OF DRURY LANE

The Biography of a Theatre Manager

Paul Sawyer, Ph.D.
Professor of English
Bradley University

UNIVERSITY
PRESS OF
AMERICA

LANHAM • NEW YORK • LONDON

University Press of America,® Inc.

4720 Boston Way
Lanham, MD 20706

3 Henrietta Street
London WC2E 8LU England

Library of Congress Cataloging in Publication Data

Sawyer, Paul, 1920-
Christopher Rich of Drury Lane.

Bibliography: p.
Includes index.
1. Rich, Christopher, d. 1714.   2. Drury Lane
Theatre.   3. Theater—England—London—History—17th
century.   4. Theatrical managers—Great Britain—
Biography.   I. Title.
PN2598.R457S29   1986   792'.023'0924   [B]   86-13203
ISBN 0-8191-5499-7 (alk. paper)

𝒸𝓁

All University Press of America books are produced on acid-free
paper which exceeds the minimum standards set by the National
Historical Publications and Records Commission.

829594

Dedication

To my mother who nurtured my intellectual development and to
my wife who encouraged me to apply it in this and other scholarly
labors.

Acknowledgements

I wish to express my gratitude to:

Bradley University for granting me two sabbatical leaves, one of which I spent in England researching and the other in my office writing; the university's Board for Research and Creativity for several sums of money which enabled me to obtain various necessary materials, and to defray the cost of preparing this manuscript for reproduction;

The American Philosophical Society for grants which enabled me to visit England on two other occasions;

The Folger Shakespeare Library and the Huntington Library for fellowships which enabled me to enlarge my research.

Table of Contents

Chapter I
From Somerset to London (1647-1694)

There are at least four fairly substantial reasons for writing a biography of Christopher Rich. The most substantial is that
he played a significant role in the development of London's
theatrical entertainment for almost seventeen years (1693 to 1709)
as the manager of the Theatre Royal in Drury Lane. The next most
substantial is his influence, both genetically and environmen-
tally, upon his son John, who as a pantomimist and theatre manager
(Lincoln's Inn Fields and Covent Garden) greatly affected the London stage from 1714 until his death in 1761. The next two are
somewhat related: much information about Christopher Rich needs to
be corrected and he has never been the subject of an even modestly
detailed study. For example, Colley Cibber's brilliant portrait
of him in his Apology as a sinister, sometimes comic, lawyer lurk-
ing in the backstages of Drury Lane and Dorset Garden is clearly
one-sided; whereas Joseph Knight, in his three-column account of
Rich in the Dictionary of National Biography written at the turn
of the century, does not even venture at a circa for Christopher's
date of birth, does not mention his place of birth, the family he
sprang from or produced, and makes several unfortunate errors of
fact and interpretation. If the reader deems these reasons too
inconsequential for writing a biography, then I have wasted my
time. I think I have not.

    Probably sometime in the 1500's, but certainly in the very
early 1600s, Christopher Rich's ancestors were living in Over
Stowey, Somerset. Since the Over Stowey registers, now housed in
the Somerset Record Office, Taunton, begin in 1558, it seems reasonable to assume that the Riches were not members of the Over
Stowey parish much before 1607, the date of the first entry bearing the name Rich in the registers.[1] It cannot be definitely
ascertained that members of the family had moved into the area at
the time or that they had recently converted to Anglicanism. But
whether as a result of an act of body or mind, the Riches begin to
appear regularly in the rather sparsely populated registers.
Three men named Rich--Edward, Samuel, and Francis--father 13
entries between 1608 and 1626. Possibly they were brothers and
possibly one of them was the grandfather of Christopher. But
which one? We have to work with the very limited knowledge that
Christopher was baptized on December 30, 1647 and was the son of
John and Susanna Rich. The Over Stowey registers tell us that,
and the Gray's Inn Admission Register, 1521-1887, informs us that
Christopher was John's second son. From various entries in the
Over Stowey registers we know that Christopher's father and mother
were probably producing children as early as 1633, and definitely
as early as 1635. Therefore it follows that John was in his very

1

late teens or older at the birth of their first child, and hence
John was probably born before 1615. Samuel, who was married in
1607 and died in 1623, was the father of six children, one of whom
is named John and was baptized in 1621. This John, it is clear,
was too young to have begun a family in 1633 or 1635. Edward Rich
was the father of four children baptized in Over Stowey, among
them a John in 1626. Obviously he is too young. Francis, who
died in 1623, is recorded as the father of Francis in 1611,
Charles in 1614, and Thomas in 1623. But no John. If we had to
choose a grandfather for Christopher from among these three, it
would have to be this Francis, but on the precarious evidence of
the lack of a negative, rather than the presence of a positive,
fact. The perilous assumption would be that Francis fathered a
John before his affiliation with the Over Stowey parish was established. Of course, it is also possible that Christopher's grandfather was somebody else. It is apparent we can reach no conclusion. Genealogically fascinating as this may be, it is not of
great consequence to this biography, since we know nothing of any
of these three or of any other possible Rich progenitor.

Just when or where John and Susanna, Christopher's parents,
were married is unknown. No mention is made of their nuptials in
the Over Stowey registers, in the indexes to the printed Philli-
more marriage registers, nor in the transcripts or parts of the
bishop's transcripts, both of which cover a number of parishes in
the vicinity of Over Stowey. That their marriage cannot be found
in the Over Stowey registers is not surprising, since marriages
may be made in heaven but the banns are usually pronounced in the
wife's parish.

The first of Christopher's siblings was probably Susan,
described as "d. of John Riche" and baptized on August 14, 1633.
The name of the child, even though her mother's name is not given,
suggests she was indeed the offspring of John and Susanna Rich.
Two years later (on September 16, 1635) "John, s. of John and
Susan Riche" was baptized. Another two years (September 24, 1637)
and Catherine, identified as the daughter of John and Susan, was
baptized. About five years later (November 1, 1642) Simon was
baptized but eleven months later (October 5, 1643) he was buried.
The burial is important, since Christopher could not have been
described as the "second son" of John in the Gray's Inn Admission
Register had Simon been alive. Child number 5, Priscilla, "d. of
John & Susana Rich" was baptized on August 18, 1644. Christopher
himself (spelled "Christofer" in the register), child number 6,
came along three years later. And Mary, number 7, "d. of John
Rich," was baptized on May 19, 1651. It may be that she was the
last, but a lacuna in the registers from 1654 to 1687 prevents us
from being sure.[2]

Beyond the parish register details, the facts about Christopher Rich's family might, perhaps, be summed up in a sentence, but they deserve a short paragraph. Several times the Riches were churchwardens: Edward in 1617, Thomas in 1650, another Edward (born in 1617, he was probably the first Edward's son) was one of two in 1652, and John, probably Christopher's father, in 1651. Over Stowey being a small parish, there was not very much of a choice, but nevertheless election to churchwarden would suggest a position of trust in the community, a trust derived from character and/or means, as well as a willingness to serve. How John earned a living may never be learned, but it is probably safe to say that most of the residents were engaged in some form of agriculture or animal husbandry. How Christopher obtained an education in Over Stowey--if he did--we cannot state because the earliest school record in the Somerset Record Office is the Commonplace book begun by the master of the Taunton grammar school, Reverend James Upton, in 1704. From the book we learn that Upton was a good classicist but a lazy teacher, that he paid his servant 15 shillings a quarter in 1718, and that other Riches sent their children to the school and were sometimes delinquent in their accounts. But, of course, nary a word of Christopher.

We can only speculate why Christopher left Somerset. The challenges and opportunities of a remote county may have been insufficient to appeal to a man of his ambitions. He may have been unsuccessful or too successful in a love affair; he may have quarreled with his father; he may have sought a better education than was available at home. A relative or a friend of the family living in London may have needed the assistance of a young man in his business. Whatever the reason, Christopher departed Over Stowey in or before 1673. Whether he stopped for some time en route, or what he did immediately upon his arrival in London, is unknown. The first written record of him I have found is his presence at the wedding of Thomas Skipwith on April 30, 1673.[3] Christopher, just a little over 25, "alleged" Skipwith's marriage to Elizabeth Madison, widow of St. Giles. Skipwith and Christopher are both described as "of Gray's Inn"; Skipwith is an esquire, Christopher a gentleman. Just how they met I cannot discover, but it is clear that Skipwith was probably the single greatest influence upon Christopher's life and it was through him that Christopher wedged his way into the theatre business some 15 years later. Although a resident of Gray's Inn, Christopher was not at this time a law student. Three years later, on June 6, 1676, he was admitted to the society as a student. For many years he continued to live in Gray's Inn, and that he practiced law cannot be questioned, but it was as a solicitor, never as a barrister.

His professional activities are difficult to trace for the

3

next decade. Undoubtedly he pursued his legal studies, but for how long I cannot state. Nor can I be certain when he partici- pated in his first case as a solicitor, although he was involved as a plaintiff in a Chancery suit in 1682 (Rich vs. Berners, Michaelmas, 1682). For some time he served as Thomas Skipwith's law clerk; he is so identified in the will of Skipwith, who was knighted in 1678 and died in 1694. Christopher is one of the two executors of the will suggesting that Skipwith trusted him. Sir Thomas and Christopher were associated not only in legal affairs, but also in various business dealings of which the theatre was only one, albeit for us, certainly, the most important one.

But, of course, Christopher's life was filled with more than purely professional concerns. At some time in his late 30's he undertook the courtship of a girl fifteen years younger than he, Sarah Bewley of Eltham, Kent. Sarah had been born on Christmas day in 1662, the daughter of a merchant, John Bewley. (In the Eltham parish registers Bewley loses the second e.) Probably this same John Bewley was the father of a boy, Thomas, born on July 17, 1661. Sarah's mother's name was Sarah Evans.[4] On her 22nd birth- day (December 25, 1684), Christopher, identified as a gentleman of Gray's Inn, married her in St. Stephen's Walbrook.[5] Her parish is given as Eltom [Eltham] Co. Kent; why they were wed at St. Stephen's Walbrook instead of Eltham, I do not know.

At this time, usually, within a year or two after marriage a couple's first child would appear, followed rapidly by others, with a very heavy infant mortality. This was the Riches' experi- ence, except that more than three years passed before their first child, a daughter named after her mother, was born on February 9, 1687/88. She was baptized on March 1. The St. Giles in the Fields register, which records the birth, describes Christopher as a "gentleman" residing in Gray's Inn. Unfortunately, little Sarah lived fewer than two years. She died on January 21, 1688/89 and was buried three days later--not at St. Giles, but rather at Elt- ham, in whose parish registers the death is listed. Had the Riches changed their residence? Had they quarreled and separated? Or had Sarah, burdened with a sickly child and enceinte with another, returned for a time to the bosom of her family? Did she and Christopher, who would later obtain a burial plot at St. Andrews Holborn, prefer to inter their daughter midst the Bewleys in the Eltham church yard? Probably we shall never know but Sarah was still in Eltham when her second daughter, Susan, was born on March 23, 1688/89 and baptized there on April 18. There are no further references to Christopher and his family in the Eltham registers.

Sarah eventually came back to London; all other references relating to her that I have found occur in London parish regis- ters. Sometime within the next two years two more daughters, Mary

4

and Elizabeth, were born to Sarah. I have not been able to find the baptismal record of their births but it is probable that their lives were so brief that they were never baptized. I theorize that the two girls were twins who survived parturition only briefly, but it is possible that one girl was born in 1690 and the other in 1691. Mary was buried on March 21, 1690/91 at St. Andrews Holborn. It is the first entry dealing with Christopher's family in the St. Andrews Holborn registers. Just a few weeks later, on April 8, Elizabeth died, the same registers reveal. Thus far the Riches had lost three of their first four children. Undoubtedly the oft-bereaved parents welcomed the advent of their first child and first boy, destined to become a prominent figure in the 18th century English theatre, John, who was baptized at St. Andrews Holborn on May 19, 1692.[6] In all these entries Christopher is described as "of Gray's Inne" and sometimes as a "gentleman." John was followed by another boy, Christopher Mosier, destined to occupy a much less prominent place in that same theatre; he was baptized at St. Andrews Holborn 14 months after John, on July 6, 1693. These are the only two children of Christopher to survive him. For some reason none of the girls' lives could be sustained. The next, and last, child born to Christopher and Sarah was Catherine, who was christened at St. Giles on September 16, 1694 and buried only two days later. Shortly afterwards Sarah Rich herself died, and was interred on October 18, 1694. One has to wonder whether Sarah's death was not a result of complications resulting from Catherine's birth. Or, she may very well have been exhausted, having borne seven children in seven years. Sarah, described as "from High Holborn," was buried in the churchyard at St. Andrews Holborn, "carried away" from St. Giles, whose registers record her death. Sarah left no will but an administration (PROB 6/70 in the Public Record Office). It does not tell us very much, but it does state that her residence was in St. Giles in the Fields, and that she leaves all administrative rights to her husband.

Thus, putting ourselves for a moment in Christopher's shoes, we are left with three children, a daughter Susan, 5, and two sons, John, slightly more than two, and Christopher Mosier, slightly older than one. Busily engaged as he was by this time in theatrical matters (as we shall see), what should he do with his children? Ask a grandmother to come to London to live with him and bring them up? Hire someone to care for them? Ship them to relatives either at Eltham or Over Stowey? Important questions, but we cannot answer them in any detail. Two months after the death of his wife he is described as living in London next to "the Eagle and Stone" in High Holborn, above Little Queen Street.[7] Whether his children were with him we cannot be sure, but at the next death in the family--yes, Susanna, the only surviving daughter, was buried on August 24, 1697, at St. Andrews Holborn--

Rich is described "from Holborne Bloomsbury." Can we say that Susanna had been living with him? Not necessarily: she could have been living elsewhere fairly close to London, and Christopher wanted her to be buried in the family plot at St. Andrews Holborn. I can locate no further reference to Christopher or his family in any parish register until his death some 17 years afterward. More of that later.

It would be helpful, certainly, if we could learn of the role played by Christopher in the development of his sons, whether they grew up in the backstages of Drury Lane theatre, perhaps made occasional visits to the other London theatres, and wandered through the ebullient fairs. It would be helpful if we could have a description of John, and perhaps of his younger brother, attending rehearsals or regular performances, laughing at the gestures of some of the comic actors, admiring the oratorical speeches of the tragic actors, having youthful crushes on some of the attractive actresses. Since Christopher Mosier seems never to have entertained any thespian ambitions of his own, it would be satisfying if a few stories of his counting the houses or checking receipts were extant--although Christopher Mosier would have had to be precocious indeed since his father's active connection with Drury Lane ceased in 1709, when Christopher Mosier was only 15. But no accounts, even apocryphal ones, exist; the brothers in their early youth seem to have had very little contact with the stage in any of its aspects. Colley Cibber, who gives us so many invaluable pictures of the father, who shared some of his social moments and knew him intimately--if we accept Cibber's account in his Apology--never alludes to the children as children at all, and refers to John only when he takes over Lincoln's Inn Fields playhouse after Christopher's death. Alas, a portrait of Christopher as père cannot be drawn.

As a businessman his non-theatrical activities are not entirely clear, but certainly less obscure than his paternal ones. He engaged in a number of land purchases, often in conjunction with Sir Thomas Skipwith, whom Christopher had served as law clerk and with whom he was associated for many years. Christopher joined Sir Thomas, as well as another man named Metcalfe, in a land development near Theobalds Road in St. Andrews Holborn parish, an eight acre plot called Gravel Pitts field near Gray's Inn. The development did not please Gray's Inn Society, which in 1687 asked the Lord Chancellor, George Jeffries, to arbitrate their differences. Although details are lacking, it is known that Sir Christopher Wren headed a committee inquiring into the matter. Finally, the Society accepted the Lord Chancellor's proposals. Some years later, on April 23, 1713, Christopher and Rupert Clarke, a close associate in many business deals in and out of the theatre and apparently a close personal friend, assigned the

6

rights they had in the Gravel Pitts field to a John Metcalfe (probably the same Metcalfe involved in the original speculation or a relative) for ₤400.[9] On the same day Christopher and Clarke also assigned a mortgage and equity of redemption or a messuage or tenement with appurtenances in Gray's Inn Lane for ₤300, another indication of Christopher's varied property interests.[10] Still another is his leasing a number of houses in the playhouse passage leading to Drury Lane theatre from the Duke of Bedford, devoting large sums of money to improving them, and then renting them out. If we believe his son John's letter to the Duke of Bedford on March 9, 1737/38, the repairs were so expensive and took up so much time that Christopher had lost money on them before the lease expired and he died.[11] There were a number of such investments in London real estate, although Christopher's chief interests lay in the theatre.

Let us now turn to his theatrical concerns. I shall first present a brief history of the two patent theatres which became the profitable passion of the last 25 years or so of his life. The two patents Charles II granted, one by privet seal and under the Great Seal in April, 1662, to Thomas Killigrew, and one in January, 1662/1663 to Sir William Davenant, were not exercised with equal success. All the vicissitudes of the competing companies will not be detailed here--they can be found in Leslie Hotson's The Commonwealth and Restoration Stage, in Volume XXXV of the Survey of London series, The Theatre Royal, Drury Lane, and The Royal Opera House, Covent Garden, and I shall mention only the outstanding developments until 1682, the year in which Sir Thomas Skipwith made his first investment in the theatre. And where Skipwith led in those years, Christopher seemed sure to follow. Killigrew's troupe, known as the King's Company, had established themselves briefly at a playhouse in Vere Street, near Clare Market, then moved to a new theatre on Brydges Street in 1663. A harbinger perhaps of the misfortunes its occupants were to experience, a fire gutted the playhouse about eight years later. To rebuild it, Killigrew was forced to mortgage his interest in the property, including his patent, to the trustees for Richard Kent. In 1674 the second theatre on Brydges Street--soon to bear the title of Theatre Royal, Drury Lane--opened, its reconstruction having cost somewhere between ₤3300 and ₤4400. In the meantime, Davenant and his actors, who called themselves the Duke's Company, had remodeled Lisle's Tennis Court in Lincoln's Inn Fields and performed in the improved theatre, now known as the Duke's. After Davenant's death in 1668, a new playhouse was erected at Dorset Garden, bordering on the Thames; it opened in 1671. There, the Duke's Company, under the direction of Sir William's son Charles, thrived. However, the King's Company, torn by sibling rivalry between Thomas Killigrew's two sons, Charles and Henry, and torn also by distrust, financial problems, dismal management, and the

7

appropriation of the company's stock of costumes--a tragi-comedy
of circumstances as embroiled as any play they performed to dwind-
ling audiences--could not maintain themselves.

It is not entirely clear just which of the two theatres, the
prosperous one at Dorset Garden or the troubled one at Brydges
Street, first proposed a union. Nor is it definitely established
that the possibility of such a union had not been discussed by
Charles Killigrew (who seems not to have consulted with other
shareholders of the Brydges Street playhouse) and Thomas Betterton
and William Smith, co-acting managers at Dorset Garden, and
Charles Davenant. In April, 1682, the Brydges Street playhouse
closed; on May 4 the two companies merged, Killigrew negotiating
(and exceeding his powers to do so) for the King's Company, and
Charles Davenant, Betterton and Smith for the Duke's Company.
What interests us, however, is an event that occurred shortly
before the Brydges Street playhouse closed: Sir Thomas Skipwith
purchased a half share of the original ten into which Dorset
Garden's ownership was divided. The date was March 21; the vendor
was Dame Mary Davenant, the widow of Sir William, the mother of
Charles. After Sir William died intestate in 1668, she had played
a somewhat ambiguous role in order to assure that Charles, then
only 11 or 12 years old, and not Davenant's stepsons, would
inherit. As Charles' guardian she had preserved her husband's 3.3
shares (out of 10) and ruled the company as patentee until June,
1673, when she yielded the direction of the theatre to Charles,
although he was then only 17. When he came into his majority in
1677 he controlled the patent as well as 4.5 shares, or almost
half of the Dorset Garden property. The following year, on
October 8 to be exact, coinciding with his Michaelmas marriage to
an heiress, Frances Walden, Charles deeded a one-half share to his
mother.[12] And it is this one-half share that Dame Mary sold to
Sir Thomas Skipwith on March 31, 1682.[13] Shortly afterward, on
May 4 as has been stated, the two Charleses, Killigrew for Drury
Lane and Davenant and his co-sharers at Dorset Garden, signed an
agreement to unite the two theatres and the two patents. It was
not, as must be obvious, a merger between equals but one more
properly described as a "swallowing alive," to paraphrase Hotson
(p. 273), with the dissolution of the King's Company, the acquisition of its playbooks and possessions by the Dorset Garden Company, and an arrangement to perform at Drury Lane (the name more
commonly attached to the Brydges Street playhouse from the
1690's). The details are neatly summarized by Hotson (p. 271) but
for our purposes we should note that Charles Killigrew did not
have authority to sign the indenture, that both companies but
especially the King's had known legal and financial problems, that
relations with actors had not always been harmonious, that the
patents were considered purely familial properties to be disposed
of from father to son to brother or to wife, and that the burden

8

of building a new theatre was shared by a number of investors rather than borne by a single entrepreneur. I make all these points in order to demonstrate that a certain pattern had been established before Christopher Rich bought an interest in a patent. Colley Cibber's Apology does not reveal this sufficiently, because not having experienced the parlous times under the various Killigrews and Davenants, he sometimes seems to imply that the numerous problems afflicting the London stage in the 1690's and the first decade of the 1700's were innovations of Christopher Rich. As a matter of fact, affairs were much better organized and the theatre was on a much firmer footing under Rich's direction. But it must be acknowledged that the Duke's Company was much the better administered and the more profitable of the two early companies, and that this company, contrasted to the King's Company, was to a considerable extent under the control of playwrights and actors. You will remember one of Colley Cibber's constant themes is that the theatre is much better off when it is in the hands of those whose business is as much on the stage as off.

Skipwith, as we have seen, had entered the theatre business in 1682 in a very modest way. Christopher himself, his interest perhaps piqued by the small investment of his employer, moved into it, also in a modest way, five years later. On March 22, 1687 (n.s.) he bought himself a 1/15 share of the theatre (not the patent) that Sir William Davenant had constructed in Lincoln's Inn Fields, entitling him to one equal share (i.e., 1/15) in the general receipts of the playhouse. For it he paid Ƚ300 5s.[14] The share was of little value at the moment, since the united companies were now playing only at Drury Lane (i.e., on Brydges Street) or (less frequently) at Dorset Garden. But Christopher must have had something in mind, possibly anticipating the time when the theatre in Lincoln's Inn Fields would reopen--something that occurred eight years later. And, more than a decade after that, Christopher himself was to take over and rebuild the playhouse.

But let us return to tracing the anfractuous path Christopher trod on his way to a share in, and later control of, another theatre, Drury Lane. In May, 1687, only a few months after Christopher had purchased his insignificant share in the ownership of the idle playhouse in Lincoln's Inn Fields, and five years after the merger of the two companies, Charles Davenant (certainly not the best of financiers) agreed to sell his interest in the theatre to his brother Alexander, an entrepreneur more active than successful. Unable to muster the sum of Ƚ2400 which he needed to make the purchase, Alexander undertook negotiations with Sir Thomas Skipwith and Christopher Rich, who seems to have been functioning as one of Skipwith's attorneys. Of course Skipwith was a

9

distinguished and veteran barrister who had held many positions of honor at Gray's Inn, while Christopher had held none.[15] Undoubtedly Skipwith could have handled the details himself, but probably he was concerned with other matters and trusted his long-time assistant to do some of the legal work. Two indentures were signed. The first, on August 20, 1687, between Alexander and Charles Davenant, transferred the aforementioned ₤2400 to Charles, but unknown to him was the fact that ₤2000 of it had been borrowed from Skipwith. In return, Charles yielded his 4/20 of the adventurers' shares, his interest in the clothing and scenes, the Davenant patent, the stock of plays listed in the 1682 union agreement, and the remaining part of the 19 year lease (begun November 9, 1682) on the Theatre Royal. Of more concern to us is the other indenture, signed 13 days later (September 1, 1687) between Skipwith and Alexander. In exchange for ₤2000 Alexander made over to Skipwith 5/6 of his share for seven years. Since Alexander wanted to manage the theatre himself--a large number of people, even today, think that no special knowledge is required to conduct a playhouse successfully--he allowed Skipwith ₤6 a week, or ₤312 a year, plus the ticket privileges which so often accompany theatrical contracts: Skipwith was entitled to two box seats, or four pit seats, or six middle gallery seats per week. At any time during the seven years Alexander could buy back the 5/6 share by paying Skipwith ₤2000.[16] All the documents associated with this indenture were delivered to and kept by Christopher but he was eager to do more than simply hold the papers in an investment which was paying better than 15% interest, and which was well secured by a highly lucrative monoply.[17] His opportunity came about 30 months later (March 17, 1689/90) when he bought the 1/6 share remaining in Alexander's possession for ₤400. The following day he leased the 1/6 share back to Alexander in return for ₤1 4s per week (₤62 8s per year), which was the same percentage of interest that Skipwith was earning, and the same number of free tickets. Alexander was to hold and manage this sixth part for what remained of the seven years (due to expire September 10, 1694). Alexander reserved the right of redemption not for the ₤400 Christopher had paid, but for ₤50 less. The deal, then, with the redemption clause, was somewhat less advantageous than Skipwith's but still good enough to content Christopher. While we are discussing the financial details, we might mention that for some reason one of the trustees for Davenant's wife, a Mr. Bolesworth, "had not Executed ye Conveyances of ye Patent & Shares as well as Mr. Betterton ye other Trustee had done" and Davenant signed a bond in July, 1690 promising to pay Rich a penalty of ₤3000 if Bolesworth did not "Execute ye same" within three months. This information comes from the Reply of the Patentees to a Petition of the Players, both documents dating from 1694, which we shall discuss at some length later. From the Reply we learn that the execution still had not been made four years after the bond had been signed, that the various contracts had been "drawn & Ingrossed" at the chamber of a Mr. Folkes and were sealed at the chamber of Skipwith's counsel, Sergeant Pemberton. We also learn that Rich paid Betterton Ŀ2000 of the purchase money by a note on Sir Francis Child, at which time all the "Writings" were put in Rich's custody where they had remained.[18]

However, Alexander Davenant proved to be just about totally incompetent as the manager of the united companies, even though he seems to have depended heavily upon Thomas Betterton's assistance. Davenant borrowed substantial sums of money from performers such as Mrs. Barry, who loaned him Ŀ600 or Ŀ800, and from putatively sophisticated investors such as Skipwith (more than Ŀ700) and Christopher Rich himself (more than Ŀ600).[19] Toward the end of 1692 and for most of 1693 Davenant failed to pay the weekly interest due Skipwith and Rich; apparently Skipwith received in these two years only one percent on the moneys he had loaned, instead of the 15% he had anticipated. Incompetence became downright dishonesty as Davenant sold the same property twice and borrowed on other property he did not own.[20] Finally on October 23, 1693 he left England and a raft of law suits, heading for the Canary Islands.

Within a month or two of Alexander's timely yet untimely absconding, Skipwith and Christopher revealed that they really owned the patent (and also the 2/10 of the adventurers' shares originally sold by Charles to Alexander in 1687 and conveyed by Alexander to Skipwith). It seems they offered to sell their patent and their two adventurers' shares for the Ŀ2400 plus the additional Ŀ1300 they had loaned Alexander, plus proper interest, but no one wanted to buy them.[21] Accordingly, Skipwith and Christopher had little alternative--one wonders if indeed they wanted another alternative--but to become managers of the united company and its two theatres, Drury Lane and Dorset Garden. They must have regarded this acquisition with mixed feelings. If they genuinely wanted a chance to manage a company, they would have one. But it is doubtful that Skipwith, who was to die the following year, could have welcomed such a new kind of challenge considering his advanced age and probably dubious health. Christopher might have thought of this as an opportunity to make a very good thing out of it, since for several years prior to 1694 the company had profited annually by Ŀ700 or Ŀ800.[22] On the other hand, they may have thought that their outlay--Ŀ3700--was too great.

I should point out here that the specific sums and percentages I have assigned to Skipwith and Christopher, although based on sound written evidence, later came into question. Some ten years afterwards (in 1704) Christopher was to assert that Skipwith had invested only Ŀ1500, not Ŀ2000, and that his (Christopher's) share was ₤900.[23] Yet in 1708 the son and heir of Sir Thomas Skipwith (who had died in 1694) claimed only a 3/5 share, and many years later Christopher's son John, in his will (John died in 1761), stated that Christopher had only a 1/6 share in the Davenant patent.[24]

Whatever share Christopher had, he seems to have taken the lead in directing the affairs of the company.[25] One reason for his doing so has already been intimated: Sir Thomas's health. He died (June 2, 1694), only about six months after the new patentees entered the vacuum (in December, 1693) left by the abrupt departure of Alexander two months earlier. Another reason is that Sir Thomas's son and heir (unfortunately bearing the same name and inheriting the title and thus creating confusion for many theatre historians) knew little about the theatre and deferred to Christopher's greater experience. In addition, the new Sir Thomas Skipwith's interests were sexual rather than dramatic. Enrolled at Gray's Inn in 1670 (six years before Christopher), he had attracted "an unenviable notoriety"[26] as a result of his insatiable desire for women and "little concerned himself in the Conduct" of the patent.[27] But it would be wrong to assume that Sir Thomas no. 2 had absolutely no connection with the operation of Drury Lane, as he claimed some years later.[28] His name is mentioned on occasion, especially in the early years (1695 and 1696), on contracts with various actors including John and Susanna Verbruggen, William Bullock, and Thomas Doggett.[29] John Dryden, writing in 1699, describes Skipwith as being master at Drury Lane.[30] Others, such as Charles Killigrew, who owned 9 of the 36 builders' shares in Drury Lane, also intervened; in mid 1694, probably about June, he promised to raise Doggett's salary after Rich and Skipwith had substantially reduced it.[31] As the seasons went by, Christopher became increasingly dominant, but we should remember that when he began his tenure as theatre manager he had nothing like a majority control over the patent, over the theatre building, or the company. Despite these constraints upon his authority, he seems to have quickly established himself as the force to contend with at Drury Lane. And the force to contend with had to contend with many forces. One certainly was financial, in part stemming from the debts the theatre had accumulated under Davenant's direction, not the least of which resulted from the large expenditures for dramatic operas. Another was the force, or lack of it, of actors, which had suffered the loss of two fine performers, William Mountfort and Anthony Leigh, which together with other factors combined to seriously diminish attendance at the playhouse.

How did Christopher and his partners face their problems? Colley Cibber suggests that Rich should have responded positively by inciting and encouraging the remaining actors to greater industry--Cibber does not go into detail. Instead, he responded negatively, Cibber complains, by attempting to lower the salaries of the leading performers, reasoning that if the upper echelon would accept cuts the lower echelon would have to follow suit (Apology, pp. 105-06). In view of the monetary exigencies of the theatre, Christopher's attempted economies seem reasonable. Next, Christopher tried to diminish the importance of the leading actors by having younger performers replace them in some of their outstanding roles. Some were willing: George Powell was quite ready to assume some of Betterton's parts. Some were not: Mrs. Bracegirdle refused to accept any of Mrs. Barry's. The more prominent actors, led by Betterton, decided upon aggressive action of their own. They joined in an association against Rich. Fifteen of them signed a petition (about December, 1694) which they presented to the Lord Chamberlain, listing their grievances in 15 paragraphs, each dealing with a different issue. In order, they complained that Skipwith and Rich had not publicly disclosed that it was their money and not Alexander Davenant's that had purchased the patent and shares, and the patentees had "Let the World beleive [sic] the Right was in Alexander Davenant . . ." and thus he was able to "couzen" Mrs. Barry (one of the company's leading actresses; her name is the first among the women signing the petition) "of 6 or 800 11 & divers others of several thousands." Betterton et al complained that Skipwith and Rich refused to honor an agreement made by Dr. Davenant to allow all the actors who were shareholders in the company Ł100 upon leaving. They complained that they had been persuaded to part with their share of the after money, worth from Ł400 to Ł500 per annum, and that Skipwith and Rich threatened to close the theatre if they did not consent. They complained that the patentees kept the mulcts (fines) rather than allowing the principal actors to dispose of them. They complained that the patentees refused to allow any play to be presented which they (the patentees) thought would attract only a small audience, thus depriving actors of their salaries and renters (of whom Betterton was one) of their rent. They complained the managers had taken the privileges they had as sharing actors away from them. Among the final eight complaints, six had to do with performers' salaries (Elizabeth Barry, Joseph Williams, Ann Bracegirdle, Suzanna Verbruggen, Thomas Doggett, George Bright). One concerned Betterton's anger about his failure to receive a promised perruque and the managers' efforts to lessen his share in the company, although he maintained his acting ability had not lessened. Another recited that the fruit money (5s per day) had been promised to Lady Davenant but withheld by Rich, and now the people who had bought the rights from her threatened to sue Betterton for it. Also, Rich was singled out for his unwillingness to pay L20 for the organ in St Bride's Church, which his predecessors had paid, and to pay Mr. Atterbury, the Lecturer of St Bride's, what previous holders of the post had been given.

13

Less than a fortnight afterward (on December 10), the patentees made a very lengthy, point-by-point response to the players'
petition. Much of it they devoted to a recitation of the various
financial dealings which resulted in their acquiring the patent.
They denied knowing anything of Davenant's promise to give ₤100 to
a sharing actor leaving the company. On the subject of after
money, they stated that Betterton and others had requested them to
take it to pay the debts incurred under the previous management,
such debts amounting to more than ₤1600. They offered to give
Betterton his share of the after money if he would discount the
salary and gratuities he had received since he "parted with his
proportion of share" in the after money. Regarding the mulcts, or
forfeit money, the patentees asserted that the purpose of the
mulcts was "to keep them [the actors] from forfeiting" for the
damage the patentees sustained, a much greater loss than the fines
paid by the performers. They flatly contradicted the actors'
allegation that the company was not performing so frequently as it
used to. They noted that the company had acted on more days under
their control than in the previous year under the control of
Betterton, who was a vicegerent for Davenant. And they insinuated
that Betterton's complaint was motivated by spite induced by the
young actors' playing, without benefit of the established stars,
almost 30 days during the summer season, which had enabled the
young actors to sustain themselves over the summer vacation. To
justify their electing not to perform on some days, the patentees
pointed out that they had to pay ₤3 rent for every acting day at
Drury Lane and ₤7 at Dorset Garden, and that the total daily
expenses amounted ₤30, and they could not keep the doors open when
daily proceeds often came to less than ₤20. Rich pointed out that
he had likewise to pay

> 3 parts in 20 of ye Cleere proffitts to Mr Killigrew &
> his Assigns And alsoe ye other Adventurers Clayming
> under Sir William Davenants patent requiring an Account
> of him for their shares hath declared that in Case ye
> Receipts do not Answere ye constant & Incident Charges
> they cannot in reason desire to have ye play house
> doors open to pay Money out of his own pockett.

They stated that they were unaware that any of the customary
privileges of the sharing actors had been denied and that the
actors had not been treated as slaves. They claimed that from
1687 to 1693 (when Davenant absconded) Betterton had controlled
the choice of plays, and as of July 14, 1693, had amassed a debt
of ₤189, which the patentees had been forced to pay. They questioned the means by which Betterton had obtained an additional 3/8
of a share and a vacation present of ₤50, and asserted that he had
"browbeat" and "discountenenced" some young actors (they cited
three actors and said there were others as well) and had behaved

arbitrarily in assigning parts and advancing certain performers.
They maintained their rights as patentees to manage the company.
They said that under their control larger salaries were being paid
to performers than ever before, and specifically mentioned that
Betterton and his wife in the last two years had received Ł10 a
week plus L6 for rent, while Skipwith and Rich, who had invested
Ł3600, had earned less than Ł30 last year.

One of the most interesting paragraphs of the Reply deals
with Betterton's complaints about his remuneration. Although he
denied that his acting had diminished, the patentees disagreed,
stating "that a Man at 60 is not able to do that which he could at
30 or 40." Previously, they pointed out, Betterton could play
four or five times a week, but now if he acts "a great parte" he
is unable to perform again for one or two days. Stressing that he
had been well compensated, the patentees noted that he received 50
guineas last year for looking after rehearsals and giving out
plays, and had another Ł50 "for his care & trouble" in getting up
The Indian Queen, which he had not yet done. One thing with
another, they said, the Bettertons received above Ł16 a week when
the company performed last year, and that he had acted ungrate-
fully in fomenting discontent among the actors and urging them to
sign a petition. The patentees admitted that Betterton had been
promised a perruque, but asserted they had told him to think of
some other kind of compensation because giving Betterton the perruque might set a precedent which would be a "great Inconvenience"
to them. They agreed that they had wanted Betterton to look after
rehearsals and give out plays (both functions had been mentioned
above) and also to

> . . . consider that new Cloaths should be necessary.
> But wee very often attended our selvs & treated with ye
> Poets & as for ye Care of Inspecting ye Receipts & dis-
> bursments in seeing all ye Rents & Sallarys duely paid
> Examining all Tradesmens Bills taking an Account of ye
> Wardrobe & lookeing after ye Theatres Christopher Rich
> took ye whole Super Intendancy thereof & hath putt ye
> Books in a Regular & Methodical way & yett said Rich
> has not had any Allowance for his trouble & care
> therein.

How revealing this information is of where Christopher Rich's
interests and abilities lay, even at the very outset of his
theatrical career. Despite the fact that he apparently received
no compensation, he was willing (probably wanted and liked very
much could be employed here) to devote himself to the financial
details of running a theatre, so little visible to the audience,
so significant in a profit and loss statement.

15

To the contention that the patentees were withholding fruit money the patentees gave a somewhat contorted answer, one which includes some glancing blows at Betterton. Of more concern to us, however, is the direct reference to Rich, which adds more support to the idea that he, much more than Skipwith and Killigrew, was the most active patentee in the management. Asserting that the fruit money (5s per day) had not been entered in the treasurer's books since last January (i.e., some eleven months ago), contrary to Betterton's allegation, the patentees explained that

> . . . Mr Rich hath been Warned by severall of ye persons Interrested not to pay it it being an Unjust charge on their shares & nothing thereof mentioned in ye Indenture of Union but a Clandestine bargain made afterwards. However Mr Rich is willing to doe what shall be Judged Right & Equitable for him to doe in this case being Indempnified therein.

The patentees vigorously defended themselves against the accusation that Rich had refused to pay ₤20 for St. Bride Church's organ and give anything to Mr. Atterbury, the lecturer. "Itt is not Mr Rich alone but near 20 other persons concerned that refuse to pay ye said 2011 for ye Organ" because Betterton himself, and not the theatre ought to pay it: Betterton lived in the parish for many years (in a house belonging to the theatre) and none of the theatre renters or sharers lived in the parish, but he paid no taxes, repairs, ground rent or parish duties, but charged everything to the patentees and adventurers. They noted that it was properly a tenant's tax, and further that Betterton should be paying the patentees ₤20 a year rent for the house, and if he did not make this payment to them they would go to law to recover it. Additionally, they questioned whether the St. Bride's lecturer, Atterbury, was entitled to a free gift. The next point they made is quite revealing. The clerk of St. Bride's parish was supplying Betterton with weekly mortality bills for 20 shillings a year "which Mr Rich can have in St Giles's parish for 5 s a Year." Christopher Rich seemingly made it his business to know the price of everything.

Anyone perusing the Reply, which is about five times the length of the Petition which provoked it, must be struck by the plethora of details: facts, dates, names, places. The sheer weight of words is impressive. The unprejudiced and unexpert reader is bound to emerge with a favorable view of the patentees' side. Even Judith Milhous, who as the author of Thomas Betterton and the Management of Lincoln's Inn Fields, 1694-1708, must look at matters from his perspective, admits that "In fairness, we should note that on many of the disputed points an unbiased legal opinion would favor the patentees. They could cite contract

16

obligations, and often precedent, in support of most of their actions." (p. 62) However, she believes that a close reading of the Reply raises "serious questions as to their [the patentees'] good faith, not to mention their honesty. . . . some of their tactics are distinctly underhanded." (p. 62) The tone of the Reply and the patentees' intractability, she thinks, "may have hardened the actors' decision to set up another company rather than deal with Rich on any terms." (p. 62)

But we must point out two very important factors that Rich et al seem to have ignored. One was the attitude of the public concerned about playgoing: it is usually going to be in favor of the actors whom they probably know and often admire, and against the patentees, whom they do not know and who are often deemed an excrescence upon the body theatrical. And the second factor was Betterton's personal relationship with the Earl of Dorset, the Lord Chamberlain--they had been friends for at least a score of years. Undoubtedly the patentees knew that the rebellious actors had strong support for a license to perform on their own. Before a meeting scheduled by the Lord Chamberlain's secretary between the two parties on December 17, Rich, Skipwith and Killigrew, increasingly fearful their monopoly was being threatened, obtained a government order on December 12 that

> . . . nothing Passe concerning the Erecting a Play house or Acting in any house Erected for representing any Comedies Tragedys or other Publick Entertainment, till Notice be first given to some of them.[32]

But the December 17 meeting settled nothing. The situation, already bad for Rich and his partners, took a turn for the worse when Queen Mary became seriously ill. A royal illness and possible death jeopardized the continuity of their performances. On December 22 acting was suspended. Six days later Queen Mary died, and the theatres were closed, not to be reopened until Easter. What with his income stopped, and his monopoly being threatened by the efforts of Betterton and the 14 other prominent actors leagued with him to obtain a license to play, efforts that were bolstered by a number of influential courtiers, the situation of Rich and his partners was grave. And if the future could be viewed as bleak, a retrospective view of the first year of their management was even bleaker. Cibber relates that the cost to Rich and Skipwith of the altercations that had taken place in the twelve months or so that had passed between their coming to power and the suspension of playing was at least Ŀ1000 (Apology, p. 107). Their profits from their first year of playing, if we accept the figure in their reply to the players, were less than Ŀ30. Hardly much of a return considering the time and money (Ŀ3600 is the figure they cite) they had invested.[33]

17

Although the theatres were idle, Rich and his fellow patentees, Skipwith and Charles Killigrew, were not. As rumors of the
possibility of a license being granted to Betterton grew more frequent, Rich, Skipwith and Killigrew decided it was time to
compromise. On February 11, a little more than seven weeks after
the theatres had been darkened, they offered to submit all their
differences to the judgment of two former sharing actors and
managers of Drury Lane, Henry Harris and William Smith, who would
make their report to the Lord Chamberlain. Betterton, however,
spurned their offer. The patentees then took a further concilia-
tory step: on March 19 they agreed to accept the Lord
Chamberlain's proposal to split the profits between the patentees
and the players and to place some of the chief actors on shares,
rather than salaries (Nicoll, I, 335). But by this date Betterton
was certain he would receive a royal license to act and was
already arranging, with the help of some 20 and 40 guinea gifts
from "many People of Quality" to adapt the old tennis court in
Lincoln's Inn Fields to a usable theatre (Apology, p. 109). On
March 25, 1695, the license was issued to Betterton and eleven
other actors. Less than a year and a half after Rich, along with
Skipwith and Killigrew, had taken over the united companies they
were disunited.

Rich undoubtedly was not taken by surprise by such a development and had recognized that soon the theatres--his as well as
Betterton's--would be allowed to open, and that Drury Lane needed
to strengthen its company. He substantially increased the
salaries of the young and inexperienced actors who remained with
him, Powell and Verbruggen each going from ₤2 to ₤4 a week and
others "in proportion," and he also tried to recruit new actors
(Apology, p. 108). Among those he added at this time or not long
after were two eminently useful performers, Benjamin Johnson and
William Bullock. During the hiatus he paid at least a portion of
the salaries of the loyal actors, who were instructed to attend
rehearsals. In addition, he or one of his associates realized the
company would need some new plays. Someone--just who has not been
identified--read and approved a new comedy, Love for Love, by a
young and brilliant dramatist, William Congreve, and had almost
signed a contract for the play when the schism between Betterton
et al and the patentees became clear and Congreve determined to
give his comedy to the actors of the new company, for which he had
designed it (Apology, pp. 110-11). In fact, conditions were so
bad that the three patentees seriously contemplated abandoning
further performances, but were afraid that if they did so the
value of their patent might be completely destroyed. And as Rich
later stated in a court case

    . . . therefore it was resolved . . . to carry on act-
    ing with all possible vigor, and for that purpose to

18

hire and entertain Actors and others, and to Endeavor
to procure the Return of all (or so many as could be)
of such as had deserted, and to use such means as
should be advised for Recalling or annulling of the
said License granted . . . by the Earl of Dorset.[34]

These were certainly disappointing and frustrating times for
Rich the manager. For Rich the man they must have been emotion-
ally very difficult too. In June of 1694 his old friend and
employer, Sir Thomas Skipwith, died; in September he lost a
daughter; a month later he lost his wife and had to face the problem of rearing his very young children, two of them little more
than babies. These personal tragedies could explain, perhaps, why
he did not always show as much consideration toward the actors as
he might have. So many deaths might also have led him to consider
the wisdom of insurance, for we know that on May 11 and July 7,
1694 he purchased two annuities on the life of Christopher Mosier,
not yet one year old. Each annuity was to pay ₤12 yearly issuable
by the Royal Exchequer arising from the duties collected from the
tunnage of beer and ale.[35] One wonders why Rich did not take out
a similar policy for John. Of course he may have, but I have
found no record of it. How much Rich paid for these annuities is
not mentioned, but it would seem that despite his asseverations
about the losses sustained in the management of Drury Lane he was
not without enough money to make a good investment. The annuities
were to come in handy about 20 years later (in 1717) to make good
a large debt Rich's two sons had incurred.

Finally, more than three months after the moratorium was
imposed, the theatres opened again. Rich's decimated company was
the first to perform, returning to the boards, probably on April
1, with Aphra Behn's Abdelazar; or, The Moor's Revenge. As might
be expected, a new play, a chance to see a largely new company,
and all those months of dramatic deprivation attracted a large
crowd. More typical was the second night, when a very skimpy
audience turned out, owing in part to the lamentable fact that
Abdelazar was not very much of a play and the acting, we can
assume, was mediocre for, as an observer was to state a few years
later, with the old actors went "the very beauty and vigour of the
Stage," and those left behind were "for the most part Learners,
Boys and Girls, a very unequal match for them who revolted."[36]
Succeeding attractions that month--we cannot be sure what they
were but it is possible John Dryden and Sir Robert Howard's The
Indian Queen was revived--were not very popular. Rich could do
little but wait despondently for Lincoln's Inn Fields to open,
which it did on April 30. The few pounds his 1/15 interest in the
playhouse would generate was as nothing compared to losses he
would undergo as a result of the new company's taking away so much
of his potential audience. What must have hurt Rich particularly

19

was their opening play, Congreve's <u>Love</u> <u>for</u> <u>Love</u>, which his theatre had tried so hard to obtain. It was (and is) an outstanding
comedy and might well have succeeded had it been only half as good
as it was since it was so splendidly acted, especially by Thomas
Doggett as Ben. Further, the town was so prepossessed in
Betterton's company's favor that "before a Word was spoke, each
Actor was clapt for a Considerable Time."[37] It ran for 13 nights
and clearly confirmed what Rich must have feared: the patentees
and their two theatres were laboring under a formidable disadvantage.

Notes
CHAPTER ONE: From Somerset to London

[1]I have myself searched the Over Stowey registers. My labors were supplemented by the staff of the office of the County Archivist, who at the time of my search in 1972 was I. P. Collis. I am particularly indebted to the Assistant County Archivist, Derek M. Shorrocks.

[2]Missing among all this progeny is Henry Rich, almost certainly a close relative of Christopher. His name appears not infrequently in documents relating to Christopher and to his son John in the type of connection indicating a blood relationship. He seems to be performing the services one would expect either of a brother or close cousin to Christopher, or an uncle to John. I have found no newspaper reference to his death. He seems to have left no will in the PRO.

[3]See Allegations for Marriage Licenses issued from the Faculty Office of the Archbishop of Canterbury at London, 1543 to 1689. Extracted by Col. Joseph Lemuel Chester, ed. Geo. J. Armytage (London, 1886), p. 126. This is volume 24 of the Harleian Society Publications.

[4]See Allegations for Marriage Licenses issued by the Vicar-General of the Archbishop of Canterbury, July 1679 to June 1687. Edited by George J. Armytage (London, 1890). Sarah Bewley is described as a spinster, about 21, of Eltham, Kent "with consent of her mother Mrs. Sarah Evans alias Bewley at St Christopher nr the Stocks, Lond." The allegation is dated December 24, 1684. This volume of Allegations is no. 30 in the Harleian Society Publications.

[5]See The Registers of St. Stephen's Walbrook and of St. Benet Sherehog, London. Ed. W. Bruce Bannerman and Major W. Bruce Bannerman. Part I. (London: 1919). This is Vol. XLIX for the Year 1919 of the Publications of the Harleian Society.

[6]Many theatre historians and editors of eighteenth-century English literature anthologies continue to list John's date of birth as c. 1682, although some 30 years ago (before I had located his birth in a parish register) I had shown that he must have been born c. 1692. See my article "The Date of John Rich's Birth" in Theatre Notebook, Jan.-March, 1954, p. 48.

[7]See State Papers Domestic Entry Book 74, p. 20, part of Calendar of State Papers, Domestic Series 1694-1698, dated Dec. 12, 1694, Whitehall.

[8]Francis Cowper, A Prospect of Gray's Inn (London: Stevens & Sons, 1951), p. 79.

[9]See Middlesex Land Records, 1715/2/1.

[10]See Middlesex Land Records, 1715/2/2.

[11]See the holographic letter in the Greater London Record Office, E/BER/CG/E8/10/1.

[12]See Leslie Hotson, The Commonwealth and Restoration Stage (1928; rpt. New York: Russell & Russell, 1962), p. 236. Most of the details summarized here can be found in Hotson, chapters V, VI, passim.

[13]Hotson, p. 284.

[14]See the somewhat complicated tri-partite indenture B. L. Add. Ch. 9301. Rich purchased a share owned by John Roffey of St. Clements Danes, who had been one of the original theatre share-holders, and had paid ₤350 4s. on June 28, 1665. It is possible that Rich bought the share on March 22, 1688 (n.s.), not 1687 (o.s.) But since provision was made for buying back the share from Rich for ₤309 on September 24, 1687, I have to assume Rich's purchase was made in 1687.

[15]Skipwith had been called to the ancients on Nov. 21, 1662, admitted to the Bench on April 17, 1668, and elected a reader on April 27, 1670. We know too that he was knighted in 1673 and made a sergeant in 1675. See Raymond J. Fletcher, The Pension Book of Gray's Inn (London: 1910), I, 444, and II, 9.

[16]Hotson, pp. 285-286; The Theatre Royal, Drury Lane and The Royal Opera House, Covent Garden, Vol. XXXV of Survey of London, general ed. F.H.W. Sheppard (London: The Athlone Press, University of London, 1970), p. 3. The details are based on PRO C8/348/95 and Add. Ch. 9299 in the British Library.

[17]Hotson, p. 288, basing his judgment on Chancery Reports, Vol. 246 (1693), says that the company's average annual profit from May 4, 1682 to August 3, 1692 exceeded ₤1850.

[18]The Petition of the Players and the Reply of the Patentees can both be found in PRO L.C. 7/3. They are most conveniently accessible as Appendix A and Appendix B (pp. 225-248) in Judith Milhous's Thomas Betterton and the Management of Lincoln's Inn Fields, 1694-1708 (Carbondale, Illinois: Southern   Illinois University Press, 1979). See pp. 60-66 for a good discussion of both the Petition and the Reply. The two documents are summarized

in some detail by Allardyce Nicoll, A History of English Drama, 1660-1900, 4th ed. (Cambridge: Cambridge University Press, 1961), I, 368-379.

[19]L.C. 7/3.

[20]See Hotson, p. 293.

[21]L.C. 7/3 and Nicoll, I, 373.

[22]See PRO C7/364/8.

[23]See Hotson, p. 293, based on PRO C/5/284/40.

[24]See PRO C8/481/66. Rich's will can be found in an appendix of this volume. The Theatre Royal. . . Covent Garden, p. 3, discusses these different fractional claims.

[25]See PRO C10/261/51. This case, one of many attempts by Drury Lane's building shareholders to obtain rent due them, is dated 1702 and 1703.

[26]Fulwar Skipwith, A Brief Account of the Skipwiths of Newbold, Metheringham, and Prestwould (Tunbridge Wells: 1867), p. 29.

[27]Colley Cibber, An Apology for the Life of Colley Cibber, ed. B.R.S. Fone (Ann Arbor: The University of Michigan Press, 1968), p. 120.

[28]See his separate answer in PRO C10/261/51 February, 1702/3, referred to by Hotson, p. 306. Skipwith asserts he had nothing to do with the management, having entrusted it to Rich.

[29]He signed articles of agreement with John and Susanna Verbruggen on April 10, 1695; with William Bullock on April 15, 1695; and with Thomas Doggett on April 3, 1696. See L.C. 7/3. These three articles are summarized by Nicoll, I, 382-384.

[30]See The Letters of John Dryden, ed. C.E. Ward (Durham, No. Carolina: 1942), p. 133. Part of this letter is quoted by William Van Lennep, ed., The London Stage, 1660-1800, Part 1: 1660-1700 (Carbondale, Illinois: Southern Illinois University Press, 1965), p. 508.

[31]See L.C. 7/3, the petition of the players, circa Dec., 1694, summarized by Nicoll, I, 370 and printed by Milhous, pp. 225-229.

[32]See PRO 44/74/2. Milhous (p. 66) prints this order in its entirety.

[33]See Article 6, L.C. 7/3, Reply of the Patentees. Also see Milhous, pp. 237-238, and Nicoll, I, 375.

[34]See PRO C10/297/57. Hotson, pp. 299-300, quotes parts of this.

[35]See BL Add Ch. 9305. The annuities bore numbers 432 and 1005.

[36]A Comparison Between the Two Stages, ed. Staring B. Wells (Princeton: 1942), p. 7.

[37]Charles Gildon, The Lives and Characters of the English Dramatick Poets (London: 1699), p. 22. See also John Downes, Roscius Anglicanus, ed. Montague Summers (London: n.d.), pp. 43-44, for a statement on the reception of the play.

CHAPTER TWO
Rich the Full-Fledged Manager (1695-1709)

Let us now examine the theatrical seasons largely in a chronological order from Rich's own perspective. In 1695-1696, a season where it became quite clear that Rich was the dominant patentee, he had certain advantages over his rivals: a much stronger financial situation, a greater stock of scenery, costumes and mechanical equipment, and two usable theatres, both superior to the one in Lincoln's Inn Fields. In addition, the central management was lodged in his hands and was largely unchallenged. But he was competing against an experienced and admired troupe led by a trio of superlative performers, Betterton, Mrs. Barry and Mrs. Bracegirdle, supplemented by a corps of other excellent actors. Recognizing his own lack of expertise in stage (not box office) matters, he hired an experienced performer, Captain Philip Griffin, as a kind of general manager.[1] It is not clear just what Griffin did, but whatever it was it did not include--at least not for very long--conducting rehearsals, for that task belonged to another member of Rich's company, George Powell, an actor of considerable talent but cursed with an equally considerable attraction to the bottle. Griffin was to serve in his capacity for about four seasons while Powell continued to direct rehearsals until 1702. Rich, aware of his company's inferiority, sought to appeal by presenting a large number of new entertainments: Drury Lane staged 15, mostly original plays and one or two adaptations, to only 9 at Lincoln's Inn Fields. Among the playhouse's offerings were the two outstanding plays of the season, Thomas Southerne's memorable Oronooko and Colley Cibber's first dramatic offspring, sometimes referred to as the first of the English sentimental comedies, Love's Last Shift. It would be greatly to Rich's credit if I could say that he was so open to everyone that Cibber, a relatively insignificant member of the Drury Lane company, simply read Rich his new play and Rich had the good sense to recognize its promise. But it was more difficult than that. Cibber first had to persuade Southerne, an established playwright, to listen to the play, and it was Southerne's recommendation that led to its production sometime in January (Apology, p. 118). Several lesser plays suffered because of poor productions one might expect from such a young group of actors. "Many accidents" contributed to "the ruin" of Thomas Scott's The Mock-Marriage in September, reports Scott himself, a not unprejudiced observer.[2] Colley Cibber, probably somewhat prejudiced himself, stated that the play enjoyed "pretty good Success, for the Season of the Year, considering it the first Essay by a Young Writer, unacquainted with the Town."[3] Thomas D'Urfey's The Comical History of Don Quixote, the third part, was more adversely affected in its November production at Dorset Garden. In the preface to the printed play

D´Urfey complains that the play was hurried to the stage, that there were "Accidents," that the music as imperfectly performed, that the dancers were poor, and that a puppet show was placed so far from the audience that the words of the "Prolocutor" and the puppets could not be heard.[4] Surely a revealing and damning list of deficiencies. Other plays met with factions (Aphra Behn´s The Younger Brother) and "prejudic´d Gentlemen" interrupted Robert Gould´s The Rival Sisters.

But Lincoln´s Inn Fields had its share of problems too, even though Cibber, whose sense of time sometimes fails him, wrote that "Success pour´d in so fast upon them at their first Opening that every thing seem´d to support it self . . . ." (Apology, p. 126) In fact, its first play of the season failed and it is likely that Drury Lane´s action contributed to the failure. On the same night that a new comedy, She Ventures and He Wins, made its debut-- sometime before September 19--Rich´s company, as the prologue to She Ventures and He Wins announces, had "out of spite,/ Trump´d up a Play upon us in a Night." I interpret this to mean that Better- ton and his colleagues did not expect Rich to stage a new play, which was, by the way, Scott´s The Mock-Marriage. If indeed it was got up in a night, as the prologue intimates, then it is easy to understand the "Accidents" of which Scott complains. But surely the phrasing is hyperbolic; the play might have been got up hurriedly, and the Lincoln´s Inn Fields troupe might not have known about it, but it is obvious a play requires more than one night´s preparation. An entry in a manuscript news report attached to The Post Boy for 17-19 September, and itself bearing a date of September 19, states, "The new playhouse in Lincoln Inn Fields is Shut up the last new play Not taking bro[t]. in by Mrs. Barry called She Ventures and he Wins."[5] Not a very auspicious opening for a new season. Betterton and his company also had to cope with the illness and subsequent death of an actor, William Smith, during the first run of Cyrus the Great, a play by John Banks, as well as the failure of a pretty good play, The She Gal- lants, by George Granville, because of a few supposedly offensive lines. (Van Lennep, pp. 456-57)

The 1695-96 season also provides two conflicting accounts of Rich´s relationships with his employees. The first was an alter- cation between Rich and Philip Cademan, Davenant´s stepson, and places Rich in a very poor light. Cademan, while acting in a play for the Duke´s Company at Dorset Garden in 1673, had been wounded in the eye by a foil in the hands of a fellow actor, Henry Harris. Cademan´s brain had been touched and he had lost his memory, his power of speech, and the use of his right side. Incapable of act- ing any longer, Cademan, like some other actors disabled by sick- ness or a similar misfortune, had received his salary for many years. When Rich came into control he decided that Cademan ought to do something to earn his salary and ordered him to "deliver out" tickets. Cademan did so until he became sick in 1695. When he was better and offered to return to his job, Rich refused to allow him to do so and thereafter would not pay Cademan's salary.[6] I have not found any explanation by Rich of what many would term inhumane behavior, but he may have felt it was necessary to cut every corner in a theatre whose financial position was so precarious. Contrast this to his conduct toward George Powell, a gifted, bibulous actor who supervised rehearsals for Rich's company. In an epistle dedicatory to a play Powell may have written, The Cornish Comedy, which was given its first performance at Drury Lane sometime in June of this season, Powell complimented Rich. He laid it on so thick that we have to ask how much is sycophancy and how much is truth. Wrote Powell, "You are so much the Gentleman (a Name that includes all Titles) in your Candour and Goodness, and the Conduct of Your whole Administration amongst us, that nothing but the highest Ingratitude can play the Infidel with You."[7] It is obvious that Rich, like so many of us, did not treat everyone equally. Perhaps the discrepancy arose, in this case, from his need for Powell's assistance.

Lest it be thought that Rich single-handedly ran Drury Lane at this time, I should point out that Skipwith occasionally dealt with the actors. When Thomas Doggett, a fine comedian and perennial malcontent who together with William Bowen had led a brief rebellion at Drury Lane in the fall of 1693, left the Lincoln's Inn Fields company in the spring of this season, on April 3, 1696 he signed Articles of Agreement to join Drury Lane, not with Rich but with Skipwith.[8] A few months later, in September, it was he who bore the brunt of a verbal attack from a member of the Drury Lane Company, John Verbruggen. Verbruggen, we are informed in a Lord Chamberlain's order, "hath with reproch full & scandalous words & speeches abused Sir Thomas Skipwith Baronet," and was temporarily forbidden to act in any theatre.[9]

It may have been in this season--Cibber, from whom we obtain the account, is often hazy on his dates--that Rich introduced a practice that was to be followed for many, many years on the English stage: the actors' benefit system. Because of insufficient revenues, Rich was often forced to pay his performers "half in good Words and half in ready Mony." (Apology, p. 218) Accordingly, Rich proposed a benefit and although the actors had contracts, many "were too poor, or too wise to go to Law with a Lawyer," and chose instead to accept this means to make up part or all of their arrears. Cibber informs us that Rich found the hopes of benefit kept the actors from mutinying. Eventually benefits became so advantageous that they were the chief article in every actor's agreement. (Apology, p. 218) Some years later the benefits were getting to be so profitable for the actors that Rich determined to lop off a part of them. But I am getting ahead of my story.

The 1696-97 season was a difficult, but not totally discouraging one for Rich. Again Drury Lane presented more new productions than Lincoln's Inn Fields--12 to 7--some of which were well received, but often the opposition's were too. In the third month of the new season the mixture at Lincoln's Inn Fields of Edward Ravenscroft's The Anatomist with Peter Motteux's The Loves of Mars and Venus proved so popular that one observer wrote that Drury Lane, "which has no company at all," needed to be revived by a new play or "they must break."[10] Fortunately a new play did arrive: The Relapse by John Vanbrugh, an outstanding comedy which has survived to this day. But a few months later, Congreve, a staunch supporter of Lincoln's Inn Fields, gave it The Mourning Bride, whose run of 13 consecutive nights to fine audiences made it one of the greatest hits the London stage had known up to that time. Drury Lane also offered Aesop I and II by John Vanbrugh, an exceptionally prolific playwright, only to have him present an even better and more memorable comedy, The Provoked Wife, to the rival playhouse. This was particularly provoking to the patentees because Vanbrugh preferred to have Drury Lane produce his play out of a sense of indebtedness to Sir Thomas Skipwith. Unfortunately for the baronet and his partners, Lord Halifax, to whom the play had been read, urged Vanbrugh to give it to Lincoln's Inn Fields and Vanbrugh had yielded to his entreaties. (Apology, p. 121) Cibber declares that the reputation of Drury Lane began to improve about this time, but it is evident that the quality of its productions was not always high, for James Drake asserted that Rich's company had "damnably acted" his The Sham Lawyer.[11]

Whatever the state of Drury Lane's finances, Rich chose to expend some of its funds on a type of entertainment which he favored over regular drama, the opera, and on one of his passions, theatre renovations. For Elkanah Settle's opera, The World in the Moon, which Rich staged at Dorset Garden in late June, he caused several new sets to be built, twice as high as customary, and "the whole Decoration of the Stage" infinitely exceeded not only that of any other English opera (so the notice in the Post Boy of June 12-15, 1697 ran) but in the opinion of several well-travelled observers anything they had ever seen on any foreign stage.[12] Elkanah Settle was duly appreciative. In the dedication to Rich of the printed opera, Settle acknowledges that he stands "so highly Indebted for Favours received of You," he wishes he could express his gratitude in a worthier way, and that he (Settle) receives great satisfaction because "this publick Acknowledgment of your Goodness, will be so much a more lasting Record of those grateful Tenders. . . ."[13] There was something unusual in the production of The World in the Moon because in the dedication

Settle speaks of an "Undertaker," who was given a benefit on July 1, which may have been the third performance of the opera. It is likely that the "undertaker" defrayed some of the costs involved in the production. Rich, however, apparently defrayed enough of them to win Settle's appreciation, but financially the opera seems to have been a very expensive failure. (Milhous, Tho-mas Betterton, pp. 106-07) He also decided to invest some money to increase the seating capacity of the house, which suggests that on some occasions, at least, the spectators were sufficiently numerous to require more places. He had carpenters cut down the forestage of the theatre by four feet and remove the proscenium doors to make place for two stage boxes. Then he ordered the car-penters to construct a new proscenium "flanked by splayed faces each containing a proscenium door" where the first set of wing grooves had been. According to Cibber, this resulted in some loss of proximity of actor to audience and as a result the audience was less able to hear the actors or to see their mobile features change.[14] These architectural alterations were probably made in this season, but it is possible they were accomplished a season or two later.

Of more consequence than dubious structural improvements to a company is its stock of actors. The best supply in London was then at Lincoln's Inn Fields, and undoubtedly Rich would have liked to attract some, even though he might flinch at the thought of paying them very high salaries. However, the Lord Chamberlain had issued orders on April 16 and July 25, 1695, prohibiting actors from shifting houses without permission. Despite the injunction, however, Drury Lane did succeed in seducing Doggett to join them, but it was only a temporary move. So too was Cibber's, who left Rich briefly either during this season, or perhaps during the previous one, but he preferred Drury Lane and soon returned. Some time after the first of the new year Verbruggen switched, too, induced in part by the offer of one share in Lincoln's Inn Fields and this move was a permanent one. (Van Lennep, p. 463) These early efforts at raiding did not, it is clear, help Drury Lane to any significant extent, if at all.

The 1697-98 season, so different from the two previous sea-sons in that no plays of lasting value were produced by either company, although there were 19 new offerings (10 by Rich), can hardly be termed successful for either theatre. Drury Lane con-tinued to offer poorly staged plays. Its production of Amintas, by John Oldmixon, was deficient: the author himself (hardly an unbiased judge) asserted that the "management of the representa-tion . . . was very ill contriv'd." (Van Lennep, p. 463) It is understandable that Mary Pix, who had first given The Deceiver Deceived to Drury Lane, withdrew it for a November production at Lincoln's Inn Fields. Rich's theatre's position vis-a-vis the

<u>Victorious Love</u>, which Rich had presented:

> I am blam'd [he wrote] for suffering my Play to be
> Acted at the Theatre-Royal, accus'd of Foolish Presump-
> tion, in setting my weak Shoulders to Prop this Declin-
> ing Fabrick, and of affronting the Town, in favouring
> whom they Discountenance.[15]

This discountenancing was reflected in the box office, we can
assume, and this may have been the season in which Cibber says
that Rich paid his actors as suited his "Conveniency." Cibber
reports that he himself was one of many who for six weeks of acting received not one day's pay, and for some years afterwards, he
adds, the actors seldom received more than half their nominal
salaries. But it would be wrong to assume that business was boom-
ing at Lincoln's Inn Fields; Betterton himself was facing economic
woes and he was, according to Cibber again, able to pay full
salaries only one season more. (<u>Apology</u>, p. 128) The playhouses
did not help their situation by trying to undermine each other's
performances. For example, when Drury Lane presented a new play,
George Powell's <u>Imposture Defeated</u>, no less a personage than William Congreve, surrounded by actors, actresses, and two female
dramatists who wrote for Lincoln's Inn Fields, led efforts to hiss
the play down. When that failed, Congreve was heard to say that
there was "a way of clapping a Play down."[16] Still another disap-
pointment this season was the first of several suspensions of a
company Rich managed. Rich was prohibited from playing for one
night, May 3, because he allowed John Powell, an actor who had
made the mistake of drawing his sword upon two gentlemen and
wounding one of them, to perform before the matter was settled.[17]
And there was one further blow to both Rich and Lincoln's Inn
Fields this season when Jeremy Collier wrote <u>A Short View of the
Immorality and Profaneness of the English Stage</u>. One of the most
withering and influential attacks upon the drama, <u>A Short View</u>
probably accelerated the movement of both theatres to the less
literary and less cerebral entertainments of music, dancing, and
other non-verbal activities. It was a movement which, as Cibber
suggests, Rich had little interest in opposing, since his concern
was to attract audiences, no matter what the means.

In such a stressful season Rich introduced one or perhaps two
other innovations, neither as significant as the benefit system,
in an attempt to make his playhouse more popular and earn a few
more pounds. Rich, Cibber tells us, had been angered by the partiality that the higher levels of society displayed toward
Lincoln's Inn Fields. If he could bring the servants into his
theatre, he reasoned, perhaps they might tell their masters about
the performances. And they could provide a little sound support

for his actors, to compensate for the often thin and silent pit and boxes. Whatever the reasons, Rich declared that the footmen could come into the upper gallery of his theatres free. Previously they had not been admitted until after the conclusion of the fourth act. And it is probable that the applause that they thundered down from the upper gallery (many lacked the discrimination of their masters and having paid nothing would be liberal in their appreciation of the actors' efforts) stimulated the company. (Apology, p. 129) Rich also admitted--just when he began the practice Cibber does not make clear--"ordinary People, and unlick'd Cubs of Condition" behind the scenes, usually for money, although apparently sometimes they came in without it. (Apology, p. 129)

The 1698-99 season shows very clearly the decreasing importance of drama and a corresponding increase in the importance of other kinds of entertainment. And since these extra-dramatic attractions are often costly to produce, it is not surprising that there were but ten new offerings, only four by Rich. Thus, for the first time since Rich had taken over the management of Drury Lane, the rival playhouse presented more new productions than the Theatre Royal. The two most successful entertainments were operas, or operatic in nature. The earlier one was John Dennis' reworking of Tasso, Rinaldo and Armida, a tragedy presented by Lincoln's Inn Fields in December, but a tragedy whose musical part was responsible for a very large share of its popularity. It was an unexpectedly elaborate production for such a small theatre and as a result underwent some satirical criticism.[18] Two months after the debut of Rinaldo and Armida, Drury Lane answered with an even more popular opera, The Island Princess. A former maestro at Lincoln's Inn Fields, Peter Motteux took Nahum Tate's adaptation of John Fletcher's The Island Princess and re-adapted it. The financial details surrounding the production are interesting, puzzling, and revealing, all at the same time. Three lines from the prologue suggest that Rich, probably remembering his losses with The World in the Moon, chose not to risk his capital again and did not defray the production costs:

> Perhaps too, when you know we've our Pay
> At our own Cost t'adorn these Scenes to day,
> In Pity to the Players, you'll kindly use the Play.[19]

Rich made still another effort to economize when it came to compensating Motteux. As a pamphlet published some 21 years after the appearance of the Motteux version of The Island Princess on the Drury Lane stage tells it, Rich, who is titled "The Patentee or sole Governor," refused to give Motteux the customary third day benefit because Rich thought that the alterations were minor. Instead, Rich "proferred him a certain sum of money, in consideration of his musical word. . . ." Motteux deemed that unspecified sum to be insufficient and he complained to the Lord Chamberlain, whose secretary mediated the dispute and arrived at a figure that apparently satisfied both Motteux and Rich.[20] Dancers and singers were imported from Italy and France by both theatres at considerable expense. Early in the season Rich engaged a famous Italian singer, Sigismondo Fideli, and later in the season another Italian, Signior Clementine, a eunuch who had been receiving Ƚ500 a year for singing at the court of the Elector of Bavaria. How much Rich paid them I do not know, but unquestionably it was a handsome figure. Not to be outdone, Lincoln's Inn Fields hired a French dancing master, a Monsieur Ballon (or Balon), and he was given the princely sum of 400 guineas for five weeks' work. Monsieur Ballon profited even more because a wealthy aristocrat donated another 100 guineas. (Van Lennep, pp. 510-11) And this season we read that the Betterton company was experiencing hard times. The leading tragedienne, Mrs. Barry, writing in January to a friend, reported that she "never knew a worse Winter," redeemed only by the "pretty good success in the Opera of Rinaldo and Armida . . . ." (Van Lennep, p. 507)

At the end of this season, and before the beginning of the next (1699-1700) seems a good time to discuss briefly the vicissitudes of the patentees' hold on its second theatre, Dorset Garden. It should be remembered that only on rare occasions had their company played there; Drury Lane was the scene of almost all their performances. In fact, from 1695 to 1704, Rich et al paid no building rent at all, although it seems that legally they were obligated to pay Ƚ3 to the Drury Lane building sharers and Ƚ7 to the Dorset Garden building sharers for every performance, a total of Ƚ10. Some of the Dorset Garden sharers, however, felt that they were entitled to the Ƚ7 only when Dorset Garden was used.[19] It was in July of 1699 that the patentees seem to have forfeited their legal rights to the playhouse. For some time their annual ground rent payments to the Earl of Dorset, who owned the land on which the theatre stood, had been in arrears. The patentees were almost a year late in paying the 1696 rent to Dorset's agent, a Mr. Shepheard. It is not surprising that very late in 1697 Rich et al learned that they would be granted no more credit. Dorset obtained a court order requiring them to vacate the playhouse. In July, 1698, after the patentees failed to obey the eviction order, Dorset "caused an entry to be made" and stationed someone at the theatre to watch it. In Easter term, 1699, the Court of King's Bench heard the case and decided in favor of Dorset. Rich's company apparently gave its last performance at Dorset Garden on July 19, 1699--the last for about seven years. About five months later Rich signed another agreement with Dorset to renew the lease at

32

the same rent, contingent upon Rich's paying what he owed, but he seems not to have done this. The question arises why the Lincoln's Inn Fields company did not leave its cramped quarters and move to Dorset Garden. The Earl was a long-time friend of Betterton and had the legal right to allow the sharers in the building (distinct from the ground, which Dorset owned) to rent it to the newer company. There are four explanations: one, Dorset Garden was in poor condition and needed repairs; two, the Lincoln's Inn Fields company lacked the money to make those repairs; three, at the time the company was in "a state of demoralized disorganization," as Judith Milhous (Thomas Betterton, p. 121) phrases it; and four, it is possible that Betterton and his colleagues envisioned the possibility of their obtaining a lease on an even better theatre, Drury Lane. More about explanation number four later.

The 1699-1700 season was a particularly interesting and revealing one for us, telling much about the rivalry between the two theatres and the popularity of non-dramatic entertainments; in this season's account I shall also include some personal as well as professional details about Rich's life, most of them drawn from the primary source of information about him, Cibber's Apology. At this time it becomes clear that the Theatre Royal has turned the corner, that it is clearly the more prosperous house, and we can determine this from several facts. Of course it would be most useful to have access to the account books of both theatres, which are available for many seasons later in the century, but we lack the data they would contain, the most significant evidence of success or failure. Frequently, one way to judge who is winning the battle of the box office (frequently, I say, not always) is the number of new productions: Lincoln's Inn Fields offered 10 to Rich's 8. Among the ten were two new Shakespeare alterations, Henry V and Measure for Measure. They were sufficiently popular to motivate Drury Lane to counter with a new Shakespeare adaptation of its own, Cibber's well known Richard III, and (if we follow the analysis of the sophisticated author of A Comparison Between the Two Stages) to revive three plays by Shakespeare's rival,[20] Ben Jonson: Volpone, The Alchemist, and The Silent Woman. The most celebrated of the new plays Lincoln's Inn Fields presented was Congreve's The Way of the World, one of the greatest comedies in the English language. But as is well known, it did not enjoy a reception commensurate with its quality. Whether it was "too Keen a Satyr," as John Downes observed,[21] or it lacked an immediately comprehensible plot,[ ] or it concerned itself with the "fantastical part of the world,"[22] it did not draw nearly so well as George Farquhar's The Constant Couple, or, as it was frequently called, A Trip to the Jubilee, which Rich presented. He must have rejoiced as crowds flocked to see one of the most lovable and popular characters in English comedy, Sir

33

Harry Wildair. In December the theatres competed directly (and uneconomically) with each other by staging two versions of the Iphigenia story in the same week: John Dennis´ Iphigenia at Lincoln´s Inn Fields and Abel Boyer´s Achilles; or, Iphigenia in Aulis at Drury Lane. The Lincoln´s Inn Fields´ Iphigenia ran six nights but "answer´d not the Expences they were at in Cloathing it."[23] The Drury Lane Iphigenia was halted after only four nights because an influential patron of the playhouse, the Duchess of Marlborough, asked to see The Constant Couple. Her request and a poor performance by Mrs. Wilkins in the important role of Eriphile combined to sink a play which Rich seems to have supported in every way. There may have been a further explanation for the two failures; as John Dryden suggested, each may have helped to destroy the other and hence they "play´d with bad Success."[24] To some extent the presentation of plays by Shakespeare, Jonson and tragedies based on Greek mythology may have been responses by the two playhouses to the numerous complaints against the low intellectual level of the miscellany of entertainments that (the grumblers charged) disgraced the stage. Thomas Brown, writing on September 12, 1699 bemoans such acts as a man mimicking the harmony of Essex lions, Mr. Clinch of Barnet with his kit organ, the inundation of French dancers, "and a hundred other notable curiosities."[25] But such grumblings did not prevent Rich from recognizing that a profit was a profit, no matter how engendered, and one of the great hits of the season was his presentation of a Kentish strongman, William Joy. At least seven times did Rich offer the feats of Joy, sometimes abetted by other members of the Joy family almost equally strong, at Dorset Garden. Rich varied the times (both the hour and the date) and the prices, charging as much as 10 shillings for a box and 5 shillings for the pit, at some performances, and at others the more or less standard 4s for the boxes, 2s 6d for the pit, 2s for the first gallery and 1s for the upper gallery. Lest we think that such biceptual demonstrations were universally condemned, I hasten to note that King William himself summoned this same William Joy to show "dexterities of strength" before the court at Kensington. Can anyone blame Rich for offering that which his monarch enjoys? Late in the season Rich was again the object of an attack berating him for demeaning the stage. The circumstances are unusual. Rich staged The Pilgrim, a revised version by John Vanbrugh of the John Fletcher original, at Drury Lane in April. John Dryden had enhanced it with a secular mask, a prologue and an epilogue. On May 1, the third night of The Pilgrim, a benefit for Dryden, the great poet and dramatist died. When he was buried two weeks later (on May 13), both Drury Lane and Lincoln´s Inn Fields were closed in respect. Rich, however, reasoning that sacrificing the income from Drury Lane for one night was sufficient, decided to rent out Dorset Garden, apparently for some ignoble kind of entertainment, probably bear-baiting. One would think that Rich might be excoriated for

34

not darkening Dorset Garden in honor of Dryden. No, he was roundly castigated by the author of The Patentee, a collection of "reflections in verse," for turning a noble theatre into "a Slaughter-house for Pence," and he termed Rich "the craving Muckworm."[26]

Several bits of evidence enable me to make a judgment about the superiority of Drury Lane's financial condition over Lincoln's Inn Fields'. One was Rich's willingness and ability to invest in a production that was not scheduled to make its debut for many months. As early as March the company was arranging for Elkanah Settle's new opera, The Virgin Prophetess, which would not appear until more than a year had passed. "Great Preparations" were afoot, the Post-Boy of May 14-16 reported, which "for Grandeur, Decorations, Movement of Scenes &c will be infinitely superior to Dioclesian [presented 10 years before] which hitherto has been the greatest that the English Stage has produced," and equal to the greatest any foreign theatre had ever offered.[27] But it would be wrong to assume that the patentees bore all the expenses of the production. At least some of the costs of the scenery were paid by the actors, for we know that six of them, including George Powell (who also directed rehearsals) and Robert Wilks, signed a contract with Robert Robinson, a scene painter, for Ŀ130 to work on The Virgin Prophetess.[28] Ordinarily, of course, one would anticipate that it would be the managers who underwent such an expense, but after the costly failure of The World in the Moon in 1697, they were reluctant, apparently, to risk any more of their capital on an operatic production (this was the last at Drury Lane until 1705) and had established something of a precedent two years earlier by requiring the actors to pay for the scenery necessary for The Island Princess. Certainly this is a highly unusual arrangement, but one which the patentees could attempt to justify by their oft repeated (but suspect) protestations of the unprofitability of their operations. Lincoln's Inn Fields, which was managed by actors who had to defray all production costs, "was running very low," in part due to the death of one of its popular dancers, Susanna Evans.[29] The prologue (written by John Oldmixon) to Charles Gildon's alteration of Measure for Measure, presented some time in February, supports the portrait of a Lincoln's Inn Fields as a theatre in dire financial straits:

To please this Winter, we all meanes have us´d;
Old Playes have been reviv´d, and new produc´d;
But you, it seems, by US wou´d not be serv´d;
And others thrive, while we are almost starv´d,
Ours you daily shun´d, yet theirs you cram´d,
And flock´d to see the very plays you damn´d;
In vain you prais´ our Action, and our Wit;
The best applause is in a crowded Pit.

That Lincoln's Inn Fields was inefficiently conducted can be gathered from a playwright's recital of how his comedy was treated there. David Crauford's Courtship a la Mode was accepted by Betterton and company but in the six following weeks John Bowman, the actor who had been assigned the leading role, did not learn six lines. Some members of the company were diligent, Crauford admits, but he discovered at the "many sham Rehearsals" that "six or seven people cou'd not perform what was design'd for fifteen." Crauford withdrew Courtship a la Mode and presented it to Drury Lane where in two days it "got footing," and "twas immediately cast to the best Advantage, and Plaid in less than twenty days."[30] This speaks well for Rich's company, certainly, but it was not always thus. Cibber states that Powell, of whom we have already spoken several times, was the "commanding Officer" (Apology, p. 113) and "a certain dreaming Idleness, or jolly Negligence of Rehearsals" infiltrated Rich's company while Powell was to some extent its director. (Apology, pp. 311-12)

Rich's relationship with Powell disturbed Cibber since Powell treated Rich "in almost what manner he pleas'd"--the servant was indeed the master, and although Rich did not like Powell personally, at the moment he did not have anyone who could replace him. (Apology, pp. 132, 139) Rich's relationship with Cibber, however, was much better. Rich seemed genuinely to like Cibber, more, in Cibber's opinion, than any other male actors. We can explain Rich's preference for Cibber on several grounds: Cibber, in his younger days, was a less overpowering personality than many of the other performers; he was not "troublesome"; he was probably less competitive, and he was less dominating in voice and height. Cibber was Rich's favorite social companion, and often accompanied Rich on his "Parties of Pleasure"; sometimes just the two of them went out together, I infer from Cibber's account, and sometimes in a "Partie quarree" [sic]. (Apology, p. 140) I assume by a "Partie quarree" Cibber means the two of them and two women.

Another reference to Rich's interest in women can be found in A Comparison Between the Two Stages. Critick, one of the three characters in this valuable discussion of contemporary theatre, is obviously hostile to both Rich and Drury Lane; he states that Rich (whose name he does not mention) is "Monarch of the Stage, tho' he knows not how to govern one Province in his Dominion, but that of Signing, Sealing, and something else, that shall be nameless."[31] It would be revealing to know something about the women with whom Rich associated--remember that his wife had died in 1694. The imputation in A Comparison Between the Two Stages is that Rich had sexual relations with one member of his company and Critick seems about to pronounce her a whore when he is interrupted.[32] It is possible that he invited other actresses to join him in the "Partie quarree." Notice that Cibber asserts he had more of Rich's

"personal Inclination, than any Actor of the _male_ [my italics]
Sex." (_Apology_, p. 140) Some actresses may have been ladies of
easy virtue, but not all: we can recall the incomparable Bracegirdle. Rich´s age (he was 53 this season) certainly would not
exclude his interest in a sexual relationship. It would seem that
if he were definitely partial to one of the actresses in his company, Cibber or some other contemporary writer would have mentioned it. At times Rich seems to have been reasonably convivial
because occasionally he used to laugh with his actors over a bottle. (_Apology_, p. 139) But except for Cibber he apparently had
no close friends among his male actors, and anyone who reads
Cibber´s _Apology_ realizes that Rich did not win Cibber´s admiration or genuine loyalty.

The 1700-01 season was largely unremarkable. Each company
offered seven new productions, the most successful of which was
Farquhar´s sequel to _The Constant Couple_, eponymously named _Sir
Harry Wildair_, which Rich presented. Neither Cibber´s new comedy,
Love Makes a Man, at Drury Lane nor Nicholas Rowe´s new tragedy,
The Ambitious Stepmother, at Lincoln´s Inn Field proved very
appealing. Much more popular was the dancing of Monsieur Ballon
at Lincoln´s Inn Fields, and Rich attempted to counter it by
introducing a young boy who was puffed as Ballon´s equal.[33] Rich
was certainly disappointed in May by the reception of Settle´s
opera, _The Virgin Prophetess_, which he had been readying for more
than a year. However it enjoyed only a brief run, in part trace-
able to its coming out so late in the season. But such a setback
was modest compared to the plight of Lincoln´s Inn Fields this
season. Several times I have alluded to the problems besetting
this theatre. Verbruggen, whose departure from Drury Lane in 1697
to join the rival playhouse has already been described, about two
years later learned how debt-ridden Lincoln´s Inn Fields was, and
Cibber´s judgment, "that they had never been worse govern´d, then
[sic] when they govern´d themselves!"[34] was confirmed on November
11 when Thomas Betterton was appointed sole manager of the theatre.[35] Indeed the situation had grown so bad a few months later
that Lincoln´t Inn Fields was reduced to presenting not only tumblers but monkeys on the stage and Betterton proposed that his
company be united with Rich´s, as several prologues and epilogues
make clear.[36] In fact, George Farquhar wrote a prologue on that
very subject, arguing strongly against it because with only one
theatre "Slavery must ensue" and poets, players and spectators
alike all would suffer.[37] Nothing came of the idea, but it seems
to have been considered a viable suggestion by at least some people. Drury Lane unquestionably was doing much better but exactly
how much is difficult to assess. Rich made every effort to
present Drury Lane as an enterprise just barely keeping its head
above water. At about this time one of the shareholders in the
Drury Lane rent, Lady Penelope Morley, attempted to recover her

37

arrears. Rich's reply was that the profits were so slim since the
creation of a rival theatre that they could not even pay for the
expenses, and that no shareholder had received any more propor-
tionally than Lady Penelope had.[38] While this was in all probability true--that other shareholders did not receive any more propor-
tionally than she--some contemporaries, and most stage historians
of the period were and are convinced that after the difficult
first few years Rich did make a profit.

In the 1701-02 season Rich offered seven new productions to
only three by Betterton's, the most popular of which was Richard
Steele's The Funeral. It had an unexpectedly long run and drew so
well that, Cibber tells us, Rich paid his actors nine times in one
week. (Apology, p. 145) We can interpret this action in a
variety of ways. Cibber, of course, does not view it as a gesture
of pure generosity (it was not; Rich owed them the money) but
rather as an effort to demonstrate that Rich would live up to his
oft-repeated promise that "as fast as Mony [sic] would come," the
actors would be paid all their arrears. (Apology, p. 145) Cibber
notes that never again during his 15 years service under Rich were
another day's arrears ever forthcoming. Fairness compels me to
point out that Cibber is inaccurate in his dating, as he so frequently is; in the 1701-02 season Cibber had only six and a half
seasons more in Rich's employ. In February Rich staged another
good comedy, George Farquhar's The Inconstant, which was distinguished by Robert Wilks' excellent rendition of Young Mirabel
but not by the play's receipts, which were substantially reduced
by the popularity of the French dancers at Lincoln's Inn Fields.
We should observe, parenthetically, that on this occasion Rich's
theatre is presenting literary drama and the opposition is answer-
ing with dancing. Neither theatre, it is clear, practiced an
unswerving loyalty to the playhouse as a situs for plays and only
plays. It may have been this season (Cibber, our source, is vague
about the exact time) that Rich seriously considered obtaining an
extraordinarily large elephant to appear in Dorset Garden productions. He was halted, Cibber relates, by the jealousy of his
dancers and, probably of more significance, his bricklayer's fears
that making an entrance for the elephant would require removing so
much of the walls that the theatre might collapse.[39] At about
this time rope dancers as well as elephants were going through
Rich's mind as potential Dorset Garden attractions. Rope dancing
was extremely popular at the turn of the century and drew huge
crowds at both May Fair and Bartholomew Fair. But on the day the
funambulists were scheduled to appear, a play in which Cibber had
an important part was on the bill. He refused to act on the same
stage as rope dancers, he told some spectators who seemed to
understand his point of view. Apparently Rich backed down, and
when Cibber was supported by other actors in the company, the
"cautious Master was too much alarm'd, and intimidated to repeat

38

it." (Apology, pp. 184-85)

Although Drury Lane's company was appreciably better than it had been when Rich took over the management, it would be naive to think that all the plays were expertly cast or performed. Many of the complaints have not come down to us, but we know that according to John Dennis, the author of The Comical Gallant; or, The Amours of Sir John Falstaffe, which premiered at Drury Lane probably in May, whoever played the role of Falstaff did not satisfy the audience, and some of its members "fell from disliking the action to disapproving the Play." (Avery, p. 19) But it should be remembered that Dennis is chronically querulous, and that playwrights are very, very seldom ever completely satisfied with the way their masterpieces are performed.

One other event adversely affecting proceeds this season was the death of King William on March 8, which forced the closing of both theatres until after the coronation of Queen Anne on April 23. However, this time Rich's company lost only about six weeks' playing time, one half as much as it had lost seven years before on the death of Queen Mary--but she was English, of course, and thus merited a much longer period of mourning than her Dutch husband.

In the main, the 1702-03 season was a vexing one for Rich. Contributing to that vexation were occurrences and non-occurrences both dramatic and operatic. Although Drury Lane presented nine new offerings to only six by Lincoln's Inn Fields, one of those six was clearly the finest new play of the season: Nicholas Rowe's The Fair Penitent, a she tragedy packed with a genuine emotional punch and good dramatic verse, but it was less successful than the very popular and now pretty well forgotten comedy presented by Drury Lane in mid-winter, Tunbridge Walks by Thomas Baker. Lincoln's Inn Fields produced more plays by the masters: four by Shakespeare to one by Jonson at Drury Lane. One advantage, of course, of staging plays by dead playwrights was that there were no third night benefits. Very disturbing to Rich must have been the non-appearance in June of a new opera, one of his favorite forms of entertainment. This new opera was described as being very "well order'd and regular" in "the Beauties of the Scenes, and Varieties of Entertainments in the Musick and Dances," and was being prepared in May. But something intervened and Drury Lane produced no new opera this season, nor can I identify any in the next. Since the author of A Comparison Between the Two Stages, writing about this time, remarks that the quality people, who love good music, were now flocking to Drury Lane and "set it in some eminency above Lincoln's Inn Fields," (pp. 21-22), the failure to offer a musical production and consolidate his "eminency" must have been frustrating to Rich. The only opera

39

given with any frequency this season at Drury Lane was The Island
Princess, originally introduced five seasons ago.

But the chief source of vexation was not operatic but liti-
gious. During the season Rich was engaged in several law suits.
Probably it was in the middle of the winter when he was the defendant in a case which suggests some of the harshness he seems to
have manifested against Philip Cademan. A little known dancer or
actor in Rich's company, John Essex, asserted that he was so lame
that he was incapable of performing a dance. Rich cut off his
salary and after 32 days of deprivation Essex filed a complaint,
also alleging that Rich had kept him from being employed.[40] Of
greater import was the succession of suits filed against Rich by a
group of shareholders in the theatre building itself, usually led
by Charles Killigrew, for the rent money--a matter of Ŀ3 for every
acting day at Drury Lane, as was discussed above. Repeatedly,
however, Rich had protested his inability to pay that rent. Killigrew, who owned nine of the 36 building shares[41] as well as owning a share of the patent itself, had cooled in his support of
Rich and Skipwith, a support he had demonstrated in 1695.[42] Killigrew and the other shareholders were motivated by several
events, in addition to their desire to obtain the money due them.
The 19 year lease on Drury Lane, originally signed as part of the
Union of 1682, was to end on November 9, 1701.[43] If the shareholders could themselves acquire a lease on the land, they could
force Rich to leave the theatre simply by not allowing him to sub-
lease the property. Additionally, "somebody"--undoubtedly Thomas
Betterton and one John Watson, a London draper--had offered to
rent Drury Lane on a much more advantageous basis: Ŀ5 per acting
day.[44] When Killigrew apprised Rich of this offer, Christopher
refused to meet those terms, upon which Killigrew and his fellow
building sharers signed a contract with Betterton and Watson, who
agreed to lease the theatre for a period of five years with the
right to renew for another eight, beginning Midsummer, 1702, for
Ŀ5 per acting day. Killigrew tried to force Rich to vacate Drury
Lane, but even though their lease had expired Rich would not do
so. According to Killigrew's complaint, Rich et al stalled,
employing a variety of legal means to increase the expense of
securing a legal order to move, and went so far as to try to persuade Betterton and Watson to terminate their agreement. Killigrew next tried to buy the holdings of anyone who had a share in
the company, hoping to obtain a controlling interest. In the Post
Man for March 5-7, 1702, he placed the following advertisement:

> If any Persons who have any Interest in the Joint Stock
> of the Playhouse in Drury Lane by any grant or purchase
> under the Patents granted from the Crown to Sir William
> Davenant or Mr. Killigrew, are willing to sell their
> said Interest, whether shares or part of shares arising

by Profits of Acting in the said Playhouse, this is to
desire all such persons to enter their names, their
lodgings, what shares they have and the lowest price
they will set at, with Mr. Thomas Hay near the Pump in
Chancery Lane, and they shall be treated with for the
same.

How many, if any, shares changed hands I do not know. About three
months after the advertisement appeared, Betterton and John Watson
signed a formal lease for Drury Lane, but the patentees paid no
attention to it. Within a few days after the lease was to begin
Killigrew was suing the patentees in court again, this time not to
throw them out of the playhouse but to obtain the rent owed by the
company for occupancy after the lease had expired. What occurred
to change Killigrew's goal from eviction to rent collection I do
not know. Possibly he realized that to evict an experienced
lawyer like Rich and Skipwith from Drury Lane would have been a
long and costly procedure. At any rate, Rich, after considering
the complaints of those joining in the suit, paid off some of
them, conceding that they were owed money, but rejected some others, asserting they had not proven their claims.[45] As a document
in the Estate Papers of the Bedford Office states, after November,
1701, Rich somehow "kept ye possession of ye said Theatre by force
against ye Wills and Inclinacions as also against ye interest of
ye said Builders, for several yeares after."[46] On September 20,
1703, Rich signed a contract for a new ground lease with the Duke
of Bedford, the old one having expired in December of the previous
year.[47] It would seem that Rich, thus armed, could have ordered
the building sharers to demolish the theatre, but that would have
been biting off his nose to spite his face. Altogether, it was
something of a coup for Rich to have frustrated the intentions of
the building sharers, who seemed to have a strong case; to have
paid only a relatively small amount of money; to have retained
acting rights to Drury Lane; and to have renewed the ground lease.
All these despite having failed often to meet the rent payments on
the theatre or the land on which it stood. An impartial observer
has to admire Rich's legal skills and business acumen, while con-
tinuing to question his ethics.

About this time Rich had to face another threat, this one
posed by John Vanbrugh, the prolific playwright and well-known
architect, who on June 15 bought land in the Haymarket and
announced that he proposed to build a theatre there which would
open by Christmas. Rich had weathered the competition from
Betterton-Barry-Bracegirdle and their cohorts, and now he had to
deal with another rival. As it turned out, Vanbrugh was over-
optimistic in his timetable, and the Haymarket did not open until
April, 1705, but of course Rich could not know that in the spring
of 1703. Although documentation linking this cause to Rich's

41

response is lacking, it seems entirely possible that the construction of another competing playhouse led to Rich's decision to revivify the largely dormant Dorset Garden theatre. The Daily Courant of May 13 announced

> The Queen's Theatre in Dorset-Garden is now fitting up for a new Opera; and the great Preparations that are made to forward it and bring it upon the Stage by the beginning of June, adds to every body's Expectation, who promise themselves mighty Satisfacion from so well order'd and regular an Undertaking as this is said to be.

As Judith Milhous (Thomas Betterton, p. 183) surmises, it might have been Vanbrugh who was considering using the theatre for operatic performances until he could erect his own, but it seems unlikely. Nothing came of it, however, much to the satisfaction of the members of the Grand Jury of London, who strongly opposed Dorset Garden's being put in regular service. About two months after the notice appeared in the Daily Courant, they petitioned the Queen not to allow it:

> we are informed that a Play-house within the Liberties of this City, which has been of late disused and neglected, is at this time refitting in order to be used as formerly. We do not presume to prescribe to this Honourable Court [of Aldermen], but we cannot question, but that if they shall think fit, Humbly to Address Her Majesty in this Case, she will be Graciously pleased to prevent it (Post Man, July 10-13, 1703)

It was in this season that for the first time we encounter the name of Owen Swiney (sometimes spelled Swinny or McSwiney or MacSwiney). On April 23 he shared a Drury Lane benefit, which means that he must have performed some service for Rich. He was, or became in the following few years, Cibber tells us, "a sort of primier [sic] Agent" in Rich's stage affairs, and seemed "as much to govern the Master, as the Master himself did to govern his Actors. . . ." (Apology, p. 177) He had "gradually wrought himself into the Master's extraordinary Confidence, and Trust, from an habitual Intimacy, a cheerful Humour, and and indefatigable Zeal for his Interest." (Apology, p. 177) Thus, he was much different in nature from Rich, but despite (or perhaps because of) this difference, they got along well together. Swiney, who was a playwright of sorts and specialized in being a hail-fellow-well-met, was to play an increasingly important role in theatre management in the next decade.

In common with the seasons before and after, 1702-03 witnessed the competition between the two theatres in extra-dramatic entertainment. Mademoiselle Subligny, a French dancer, continued to be very popular at Lincoln's Inn Fields. To lessen her appeal, Rich hired "The Devonshire Girl" to imitate her on the Drury Lane or Dorset Garden stage, and also introduced a vaulter from a "managed horse" in the person of one Evans. Also, he brought back the celebrated Clynch who could mimic all kinds of sounds with his extraordinarily versatile voice. (Avery, pp. 35, 38)   Of course there were the usual complaints about such fare, and one of the most typical was spoken by Thomas Betterton (note he was the employer of Mademoiselle Subligny) on July 5, 1703 before an Oxford University audience, whose members he flattered by addressing them as Athenians:

Then rise Athenians! in the just Defence
Of Poetry oppress'd, and long neglected Sence;
The reputation of our Art advance,
Suppress th' Exorbitance of Song and Dance
And in one Powerful Party Conquer France.[48]

The following season, 1703-04, saw no diminution in the emphasis upon other forms of entertainment than plays. Oral or written complaints were less influential than the tinkle of shillings or pence. Music, dancing and singing were often featured in an effort to attract spectators. Rich conceived (or acted upon the suggestion or example of somebody else whom I have not been able to identify) the idea of bolstering operas by insertions from other operas.   Which insertions? Those which had proved popular in the past and which were not too blatantly inappropriate.   The operas often made little sense anyway, and why let the expensive scenes and machines from previous popular operatic productions stand idle? He augmented The Emperor of the Moon with a grotesque scene and Grand Machine from Dioclesian in December, and six weeks later augmented these with the Dome Scene from The Virgin Prophetess.[49] He also invested in more expensive decoration for The Albion Queen (newspaper advertisements described them as "extraordinary Charges in the Decoration") and there were again "extraordinary" decorations for a summer production of The Emperor of the Moon (Avery, pp. 60, 72). All these productions support Cibber's judgment that Rich's "Notion was, that Singing and Dancing or any sort of Exotick Entertainments" were much more effective in attracting audiences than any company of actors, no matter how good, who subsisted on "plain Plays." (Apology, p. 180)   However, as I shall discuss later, many, many good plays were produced by Rich, equal to or better than the plays at Lincoln's Inn Fields. Rich might well have felt his judgment of the discrimination and intellectual powers of many members of his audiences was justified after the Great Storm of 1703 when there were numerous complaints

43

against Drury Lane's staging Macbeth with "his Lightning and Thunder" on November 27 and Lincoln's Inn Fields' presenting The Tempest on December 1 because they seemed to flout God. (Avery, pp. 49-50) I have found no statements of Rich's religiosity or absence of it, except for his will, which we shall examine in due course. We can conclude that Rich chose not to flaunt his belief or disbelief, which was undoubtedly a wise decision. To do the latter would have alienated even more people than his business practices had; to do the former would be difficult for anyone busily engaged in an activity which for many of his contemporaries still bore an anti-religious stigma. A more tangible consequence of the Great Storm was that it may have damaged Dorset Garden and have been the catalyst for moving much scenery from the seldom-used playhouse to Drury Lane. (Milhous, Thomas Betterton, p. 175)

No truly outstanding plays were presented this season; probably the best known today are Sir Richard Steele's The Lying Lover at Drury Lane in December and Joseph Trapp's Abra Mule at Lincoln's Inn Fields in January. The struggling company under Betterton tried many more new plays than Rich: six mainpieces and four afterpieces (one converted from a mainpiece) at Lincoln's Inn Fields to Drury Lane's three new plays and one revision.

Three other facts or events of the season merit brief mention. One, we know that Owen Swiney continued to assist Rich, else he would not have twice shared benefits with an actor named John Hall. Two, the performance at Drury Lane of Signiora Francisca Margarita de l'Epine (she had sung there for the first time a week before) on Saturday, February 5 was interrupted by one Ann Barwick, a former servant of Katherine Tofts, a member of Rich's company. Apparently feeling that Mrs. Tofts' reputation was being sullied by the Italian singer, Barwick pelted her with oranges and hissed. The following day Mrs. Tofts apologized to Rich in a notice printed by the Daily Courant of February 8, publicly assuring him that she had no knowledge that Ann Barwick would behave in such a manner. And three, Rich was one of the subscribers to John Dennis' Grounds of Criticism in Poetry, which was published on May 27, 1704. What does this tell about Rich? Does it demonstrate that Rich was much interested in poetry criticism and that he welcomed the appearance of Dennis' essay and read it carefully? Hardly. It is safe to say that a majority of the subscribers to such works, usually people of wealth or position or both, did not read what they had purchased. Rich was probably among this group. Rich's subscription to Dennis' book may have been simply a generous act to help buttress literary criticism and one of its better, if often irascible, practitioners. But more likely Rich subscribed because an author who contributed plays to Drury Lane (The Comical Gallant had played in May, 1702, and A Plot and No Plot in May, 1697) probably asked him to do so, and

44

Rich agreed as one of the necessary obligations of a theatre manager. Perhaps Rich deemed it wise to propitiate someone whose pen could be vitriolic. Dennis did give Rich his next play, Gibraltar; or The Spanish Adventure, which made its debut in February of 1705 (n.s.). That Dennis regretted it may be gleaned from his preface. But more about Gibraltar during the account of next season.

In the late spring or the summer of 1704 Rich began to make preparations for the increasing competition that the Haymarket probably would provide, competition that might be more severe because the Lincoln's Inn Fields company planned to move there. Rich had strengthened his own troupe by adding two talented if troublesome actors, Powell and Doggett, and then signed Richard Estcourt, a well known Irish comedian, and, sometime in December, Letitia Cross, a useful actress. Rich also tried to prevent the Lincoln's Inn Fields company from playing at the Haymarket by notifying the Lord Chamberlain that he would pay them "at such Salaries as his Lordship shou'd think reasonable; but his Lordship was pleas'd to declare, That Her Majesty intended to have two Companies," and he would not allow Rich "to entertain them." (The Post-Boy Robb'd of his Mail, letter 42)

This seems to be an appropriate place to introduce a discussion of a law suit, filed in 1704, which reveals much about what went on behind the scenes, the area of the theatre in which Rich, as we know, played a very significant role. Many of the details relate to preceding seasons, and the suit itself seems to have been languidly prosecuted until 1708, when the parties made an out of court settlement or the plaintiffs permitted the case to die of inanition. Briefly, it concerns Sir Edward Smith, a Lincoln baronet, who discovered upon his marriage to Bridget Bayly (widow of the attorney for the Duke's company) that she had received absolutely nothing from her one half adventurer's share in Dorset Garden since 1695.[50] This was the impetus that led him, joined by three other small shareholders, to file suit to recover the money they thought they were entitled to, claiming that Skipwith, Rich and Davenant did "shuffle, conceal, and refuse to discover" the profits of acting. They made the point, among others, that the shareholders' rights to profits included any theatre's performances not just Dorset Garden's, and that the patentees had the legal right to close Lincoln's Inn Fields if they so chose. The plaintiffs stated that Rich "hath often owned & acknowledged" that King William had not granted another company the license or authority to act, and the Lord Chamberlain lacked the license and authority to do so. Smith asserted that Rich, Skipwith and Killigrew had often "pretended" they would ask the King for redress, but kept putting it off. When Anne ascended the throne in 1702, Rich et al "prevailed" upon Smith and the other complainants to

45

advance a large sum of money to be given to a solicitor for that purpose. A petition was prepared for presentation to the Queen in Council but the patentees offered all kinds of reasons for not presenting the petition, alleged Smith. After seven months of "very frivolous excuses and pretences" they at last wholly refused to proceed any farther in that matter. The point being made here by Smith is that the patentees deliberately abstained from pressing the case against the Lincoln's Inn Fields company because they were in a sense cooperating with them. In line with this charge were others that insisted Rich et al actually encouraged the birth of the new company and that the patentees provided "occasions" of "Disgust" to the principal actors at Drury Lane and Dorset Garden so that they would have a pretext to move to Lincoln's Inn Fields, something the patentees could have prevented had they wished to. In addition, the new company had received "secret supplies and support" from the patentees, and the two companies had collaborated in selecting non-conflicting dates and plays, and had avoided direct competition especially during Lent, vacation periods and off seasons. All these were done with the purpose of defrauding the complainants "of their said respective shares and interests."

Some of the charges seem patently ridiculous. Leslie Hotson thinks that Rich may possibly have defrauded the adventurers to some extent, but "it is quite impossible to believe in any such elaborate system of deceit as Sir Edward's complaint pictures."[51] Judith Milhous agrees that some of the claims were "wildly exaggerated," but others are quite credible, she maintains, and she uses some of Smith's assertion to bolster her argument that there was an accommodation between the two companies from 1702 through the summer of 1704, during which time they shared a "modus vivendi." Other evidence to support the idea of a collaboration she adduces include the fact that there seem to have been fewer performances at Drury Lane and probably Lincoln's Inn Fields (the latter playhouse did not advertise frequently in newspapers and thus the record of its performances is less certain); when actors transferred from one company to the other there were fewer protests to the Lord Chamberlain than there had been before and after this period; there were a number of performances in which actors from both companies participated. She cites a February 1, 1704 program at Lincoln's Inn Fields in which Drury Lane dancers appeared and a masque and concert presented first at Drury Lane (February 22, 1704) and then at Lincoln's Inn Fields (March 7, 1704). She also points to an afterpiece, Squire Trelooby, which premiered at Lincoln's Inn Fields on March 30, 1704, in which an equal number of Drury Lane and Lincoln's Inn Fields actors participated and for which Drury Lane provided the dancers. Such accommodation would result in greater profits for the two theatres since there would be fewer productions of the same play at the two

houses, usually a losing proposition, and there would be less
incentive to invest large sums of money in new productions, productions whose reception were highly speculative. Only when the
Haymarket opened in 1705, she thinks, was there a rebirth of spir-
ited competition between the companies. Further to support her
contention, she introduces John Verbruggen's petition, circa 1703,
in which he asserted that the actors at Lincoln's Inn Fields were
being cheated of their share of the profits, and this idea that
Lincoln's Inn Fields was making money confirms what Smith was
alleging: that both companies were profitable.[52]

But let us return to Smith's suit to consider some of his
other points and what they reveal about Rich. Smith charged that
the patentees were making every effort to have him drop his complaint: they threatened that some shareholders of whom Smith was
ignorant would benefit if Smith's suit were successful, and thus
Smith's share of whatever profits the theatre might produce would
be reduced; and they went even further, asserting that the company
was "in debt for house rent & other things above ten thousand
pounds" and that Smith and the other minor shareholders who filed
the suit would be held responsible for paying their share of that
debt. Rich et al put up another roadblock when Smith succeeded in
getting the court to order Skipwith to produce the accounts of the
theatre kept by Zachary Baggs, the Drury Lane treasurer. Baggs
resisted, on advice of counsel, arguing that he, Baggs, was
responsible to all those who had interests in theatre, not Skipwith alone, and that the various books, papers, and accounts were
his "Vouchers." It was some two years later, very late in 1708,
that Baggs was finally persuaded to place the books with a neutral
observer so that Smith could examine them. Just how much the profits were seems always to have remained a moot point, Smith alleging (on what basis we do not know) that the patentees had taken in
more than Ł350,000 in ten years--whether Smith understood that
figure to represent gross or net income is not made clear. Rich
himself testified that the United Company in its good years was
running an annual profit of about Ł800. If Smith meant the
Ł350,000 to equal box office receipts, it was an impossibly high
figure: Judith Milhous computes that to be an average of Ł175 per
acting night, an other impossibly high figure.[53] But if those
figures are inflated, so was Rich's statement in offering another
excuse for no profits, that 60 of the 200 performance nights per
season were given to benefits--about half that number would be
closer to reality, and some of those benefits enabled the patentees to avoid losing money by having the actor enjoying the benefit pay the evening's expenses. One last disputed point was how
the profits (since there were no declared profits it was largely
an academic matter) should be divided. Under the 1682 union
agreement, Smith maintained, the profits were to be split into 20
shares, three going to Charles Killigrew, seven to the actor

47

sharers, and ten to the Adventurers, who would divide the income
from these ten in proportion to the number of shares each held.
But Rich differed in his interpretation of the agreement: three to
Killigrew yes, but the remaining seventeen parts were to be lumped
together, then divided into twenty again, apparently for equal
distribution to actor sharers and the Adventurers. The patentees
and the Adventurers never seem to have resolved this one.

The most significant event in the 1704-05 season for Rich as
well as for the theatre-going community of London was the opening
of the new Queen's theatre in the Haymarket on April 9, 1705. I
shall refer to this theatre as the Haymarket, the name by which
most people seem to have referred to it. John Vanbrugh, the chief
mover in the erection of the new playhouse, had enlisted the support of 30 "Persons of Quality" who each contributed Ⱡ100. (Apology, p. 172) He had hoped to have it ready, as we have noted, by
the end of 1703 but he encountered various delays. He and William
Congreve received a license on December 14, 1704,[54] and the company of actors led by Betterton left Lincoln's Inn Fields to act
at the "vast, triumphal Piece of Architecture" whose acoustics
were so bad that "scarce one Word in ten could be distinctly
heard." (Apology, p. 173) But months before its opening, anticipated for early in the 1704-05 season, Rich was preparing for it
and displaying a theatrical acumen that must be respected. All
the details of his activities have not come down to us, but the
immediate results speak for themselves. As early as October 28,
the Diverting-Post reported that the Haymarket was almost finished
and expected to open with two operas, both translated from
Italian, and now being set to music, one by Daniel Purcell and the
other by Mr. [Thomas] Clayton. Yet what happened? Purcell's
opera, Orlando Furioso, was never completed. And in mid-December
the Diverting-Post was announcing that Clayton's opera, Arsinoe,
Queen of Cyprus, was going to be given at Drury Lane. Somehow
Rich had persuaded Clayton to prefer a Drury Lane production, thus
seriously hurting the Haymarket. As we shall see shortly, Arsinoe
was to become a very potent attraction. But to meet the Haymarket
challenge Rich did more than steal away its opening opera. In
November and December he publicized through notices in the Daily
Courant that turned out to have little foundation that repairs had
been made in Dorset Garden and that it would soon be able to serve
for music, dancing and regular theatrical performances. Note that
Dorset Garden was not used this season, but it did pose a threat
as a refurbished theatre equipped for opera and spectacle just as
the Haymarket was. And to further hinder Vanbrugh, he attempted
to induce some members of the Lincoln's Inn Fields company soon to
move to the Haymarket to join the Drury Lane company. He was
warned by the Lord Chamberlain's secretary, Sir John Stanley, to
cease and desist.[55]

48

Back to _Arsinoe_. Rich knew that it would have to be prepared
carefully and quickly if it were to precede the Haymarket opening
and if it were to demonstrate the Drury Lane could do very well
with operas. Of course, there are considerable costs in producing
an opera, but Rich was shrewd enough to have those costs borne not
by himself, not by the actors who had paid some of the expenses of
previous operas by the Drury Lane company, but by subscribers.
Since almost all the subscribers were people of position, wealth,
and upper-class tastes, they would provide a certain _ton_ to both
the theatre and the opera, and they would fill a certain number of
seats, special ones in the boxes and pit which they received in
return for their subscription money. Also, Rich announced in the
Daily Courant that the stage and gallery boxes were to be for the
benefit of the actors. Two other features of the opera were
advertised: it would be sung in English, not Italian, which would
be likely to attract some philistines who like to understand what
they heard; and everything would be sung, nothing spoken, in other
words recitative would be introduced, something that made its composer, Thomas Clayton, think that Londoners would have to be edu-
cated to appreciate this new (for England) Italianate opera.[56]
And Rich did something else: because _Arsinoe_ was short, he augmented the evening's program with dancing by six listed dancers
"and others," as well as singing in Italian and English both
before and after the opera.[57] _Arsinoe_, with Clayton's music and
Pierre Motteux's libretto, made its debut on January 16, 1705 to
enthusiastic crowds. This first English opera, as some music historians call it, was enormously successful. It was offered fourteen times that season, not consecutively as popular plays were,
but at periodic intervals to avoid straining the singers' voices,
Clayton wrote.[58] One may question the quality of the opera--
words--but Roger Fiske thought little of the music or the
words[59]--but none can doubt its popularity.

Although his new theatre was incomplete,[60] Vanbrugh chose not
to wait until it was fully operational and introduced the new
playhouse to London with an opera, Greber's _The Loves of Ergasto_,
bolstered by a freshly imported group of Italian singers. It was
a mistake. The opera was as mediocre as the singers who presented
it, and after five days Ergasto was withdrawn. John Downes
described the singers as the worst that ever came from Italy.[61]
Vanbrugh followed it with a 45-year-old play, John Dryden's _The
Indian Emperor_, and this was succeeded by a number of the
company's stock plays, all acted in old costumes lugged from
Lincoln's Inn Fields. Not until May was a new play offered, Mary
Pix's _The Conquest of Spain_.[62] Shortly thereafter (on May 24)
Vanbrugh tried to match performances of his production of Dryden's
Amphitryon against Drury Lane's on May 16 and 18. Had the Hay-
market opened with a good new English opera, or a good new play,
the theatre veteran John Downes thought, the crowds would have

flocked to the new playhouse, but as it was, audiences fell off rapidly, undoubtedly discouraged not only by the poor repertory but also by their inability to hear well. By July Betterton and his fellow thespians were back at Lincoln's Inn Fields where the summer heat was less intense, and they resorted to such desperate departures from tradition as an all-female cast performing Love for Love, and Rule a Wife and Have a Wife with "the Principal Parts to be perform'd by those who play'd them when 'twas reviv'd in King Charles the Second's Time."[63] Another casualty of the season at the Haymarket was William Congreve, who withdrew before December 15 from the management. As Cibber (Apology, p. 176) described it, "the Prospect of Profits from this Theatre was so very barren, that Mr. Congreve, in a few Months gave up his Share, and Interest in the Government of it, wholly to Sir John Vanbrugh." Professor Milhous (Thomas Betterton, p. 192) suggests "apparently . . . he could not afford to lose money as he was doing." It was no great surprise that Vanbrugh petitioned the Lord Chamberlain to join his company with Rich's and to terminate the battle between them. Twice in the month of June (7, 21) the Lord Chamberlain's secretary, Sir John Stanley, wrote to Rich "intimating" it was the "Lord Chamberlain's Pleasure" that Rich "shou'd bring in Proposals for uniting the two Companies." So stated Charles Gildon in The Post-Boy Robb'd of his Mail, 1706 edition, from whom I shall quote at length (sometimes as digested by Professor Milhous, Thomas Betterton, pp. 201-204).[64] Definitely hostile to Vanbrugh, Gildon strongly attacks him for locating a theatre in "the Fagg-end of the Town," spending too much to build a theatre that was no better than earlier ones, failing to engage Drury Lane actors in advance, accepting advice from "those very People in the Government of this New Company, who had before ruin'd two Companies, and brought them from the Admiration, to the Contempt of the Town." Finally, he accused Vanbrugh of being unreasonable and unjust for trying to destroy and unite the companies. Rich's first response, which seems to have come in the middle of June, was a petition to the Lord Chamberlain signed by more than sixty percent of the Drury Lane actors (32 of 52) earnestly requesting him not to unite the theatre because it would be prejudicial if not utterly ruinous for them. About a month later (on July 29, 1705) Vanbrugh presented his "Proposals for the Reducing the two Companies of Players into one." Here is how Gildon lists them:

1st. That the Patent Adventurers on their ceasing to act by Vertue of their Patent, be admitted to a Moyety of the clear Profits, which shall arise from the Company now establish'd by the Queen in the Hay-market.

2d. That there shall no Regard be had to each Companies past Debts, Engagements, or Stock, their Concern together being forward, not backwards.

3d. That the Persons to be intrusted for the Management, be Nam'd by the Queen, to be at any Time chang'd and remov'd, as she shall think fit.

4th. That if these three principals Heads be agreed to, the Settlement of the inferiour Matters, may be refer'd to my Lord Chamberlain.

J. Vanbrugh

One wonders whether Vanbrugh did not realize how completely one-sided the terms were. Was he relying on the friendship of the Earl of Kent, the Lord Chamberlain, and those even higher up? Was he trying to provoke Rich into making such an intemperate reply that he (Rich) would further alienate Kent? Whatever the answers to these questions on motivation, about a week after Vanbrugh's proposal Rich sent a lengthy and carefully phrased Answer to Sir John Stanley, the Lord Chamberlain's secretary:

To receive any Persons (other than Actors, Singers, Dancers, and Performers) into any Part, Interest or Share, with the Proprietors, under the Patents, is not in my Power, without a Breach of Trust, which I cannot answer to the rest of the Proprietors, who may tear me to pieces with Law-Suits, if they shou'd see me . . . prejudice their Rights and Pro-perties. . . . Sir, I am a Purchaser under the Patents, . . . and am not only accountable to the rest of the Proprietors, and lyable to several New Debts, but also under Covenants with several Actors, Singers, and Dancers, for the whole Undertaking. And when after ten Years Employment, Expence, and Diligence, I have (notwithstanding many Difficulties) succeeded; so that the Company has the good Fortune to please the Town, and the Profits begin to reimburse, and pay the Monies and Debts contracted: If I shall now be depriv'd of reaping the Benefit of such my Labour and Charges, what must the Effect be, but the undoing of my self, and of the Interests of those engag'd with me . . . ?

And now, Sir, with Submission, I do not see upon the whole Matter, how such an Union, as seems to be intended, can have a good Effect, if one considers either the Inclination of the Quality, and Gentry, who have always declared for the keeping up of two Companies (and to that purpose, subscribed to the Building of a New Theatre) or the Management of the New Theatre, since it was open'd, which has not been such, with all the Advantages of setting forth, as wou'd invite others to put the whole under the same Government, in order to pay a very large Rent to Mr. Vanbrugh, for that which cost him little or nothing, beyond the Subscriptions received by him. And, with regard to the Players themselves, since they have already, in a Petition to his Lordship, declared themselves content with the Terms, under which they act here, and apprehensive of great Hardships, if not utter Ruin, which they conclude will be brought upon them by such a Union....

These, Sir, are some of the Reasons, which I humbly offer against a Union in general; and having on Thursday last, receiv'd Mr. Vanbrugh's Proposals in writing, I am the more confirm'd in my Opinion against it: For by the first, he wou'd have us cease to Act by Virtue of our Patents; and in the second, he declares, That no Regard shall be had to the Companies past Debts, Engagements, or Stock, and how an Union can be either practicable, or safe, with respect to the Interest of All Parties upon this foot, I cannot conceive.

Colley Cibber, in his Apology, written many years after the events of the season and subject to errors of chronology, partiality, egotism, and sometimes incomplete knowledge of the details (but blessed, from an historian's point of view, with an enviable personal involvement and a familiarity with the participants) thought that Rich should have accepted the union, "he being, then, on the prosperous Side of the Question, having no Relief to ask for himself, and little more to do in the matter than to consider what he might safely grant." (Apology, pp. 176-77) Cibber, who seems not to have known the exact terms of Vanbrugh's proposal, goes on to suggest that Rich had to consider that there were other persons who had great claims to shares, and hence in the profits of the stage, which profits would be too visible by a union and might raise a new spirit in the Adventurers to revive their law suits against him. He had, Cibber tells us, "led them a Chace in Chancery several Years," and had managed to avoid a contempt of the court citation. "He knew the intrinsick Value of Delay, and was resolv'd to stick to it, as the surest way to give the Plantiffs [sic] enough on't." In this way, Cibber sums up, Rich "had walk'd about at his Leisure, cool and contented, as a Fox, when the Hounds were drawn off, and gone home from him." (Apology, p. 177) But all this, as Cibber admits, is simply conjecture. He surmises that Rich "had a mind both Companies should be clandestinely under one, and the same interest," but in a very loose manner. (Apology, p. 178) One of Cibber's biographers interprets this to mean that Rich was not really hostile to the union, but simply wanted it on his own terms: two theatres, one for opera, one for plays, and a loose control over both.[65]

The merger plans having been at least temporarily shelved, Rich communicated his happiness to Richard Estcourt, one of Drury Lane's leading actors, who wrote the epilogue spoken at the premiere of the opera Camilla on March 30:

Our neighbors lately, with an ill design,
Strove the contending playhouse to join. . . .
But this we know, had that dire union been,
You ne'er in England had Camilla seen.
They would some masque have shown, or country farce,
Paris's Judgment or The Loves of Mars.
But since the stage's freedom you restore,
And we no more dread arbitrary power,
To please this audience we'll no charges spare,
But cheerfully maintain a vigorous war.
New funds we'll raise, and heavy taxes lay
(Dancers and singers (dear allies) to pay.[64]

The next most significant event of the season for Rich concerned personnel changes and functions. Cibber, who for the past few seasons had risen in influence at Drury Lane, helped to persuade Rich to drop George Powell as rehearsal director and appoint Robert Wilks. Rich, who despised Powell because the latter treated him with contempt, was reluctant to replace him, recognizing (in spite of Cibber's allegation that Rich knew nothing about acting) that essentially Powell was a more gifted actor than Wilks. And perhaps more importantly, Powell was willing to accept only token salary payments, and if the chief actor did so, then the rest of the company could hardly object. On one occasion, Cibber related, Powell kept the troupe quiescent, even though they had not received one day's pay for six weeks of performing. Wilks would have demanded his full salary and Rich was aware that it would have been unjust to pay him and deny others. "Mayhap," Rich said (apparently a favorite word of his), the other actors led by Powell would mutiny. But in many evening conversations with his employer, Cibber pointed out how much more diligent Wilks was, and how the example he set would have a positive effect upon the level of the company's performance. Cibber's influence was decisive and Wilks became "first Minister, or Bustle-master general of the Company." (Apology, pp. 141-42) The contract was signed on October 9, 1704, and gave Wilks ₤4 a week with no conditional deductions. Rich also provided Cibber himself with a new and profitable contract. He was to receive ₤3 10s per week for five years for acting, and another 30s per week for other services. When we read what those services are we can see that Rich recognized his own inadequacies as a theatre manager. After all, his forte was law, not the drama. Cibber's functions were to read plays, assign actors to roles and other duties for 10s a week, and to assist Rich in the management of Drury Lane for 20s a week. That Rich required the aid of Cibber to manage Drury Lane, the kind of work that takes time but hardly the specialized skills that play selection and cast selection demands, suggests that Rich was involved in other affairs, presumably connected with his work as an attorney and wheeler-dealer in various properties and other investments. Cibber, it is clear, was Rich's right-hand man.

From these actions two results can be expected. One, the displeasure of the man Wilks deposed as rehearsal director soon became evident. George Powell petitioned the Lord Chancellor to be discharged from Rich's company, using the pretext that his salary had not been paid regularly, and his request was granted conditional upon his paying back money he owed Rich (Cibber has told us that Powell had not always received full salary,· but he apparently did not know that he was in debt to Rich), and his continued acting with Rich until other debts were paid. Rich granted Powell his discharge on April 7, and he joined Betterton's (or Vanbrugh's) company. But not for long, as we shall see in the following season. The other result was unexpected. One would have thought that with Cibber and Wilks (two thirds of the famous triumvirate that was to govern Drury Lane in some of its most glorious years) helping to supervise the dramatic productions, the performances would have been exemplary. Some probably were, but certainly not all. Witness the complaint of that chronic complainer, John Dennis, whose Gibraltar, to which we have already alluded, made its debut at Drury Lane on February 16 and its exit after the second performance on February 20. Dennis, dismayed by the dismal reception, tells us in the preface to the printed edition of the play that he didn't know whether to blame "the Calamities which attended the Rehearsal, which were so numerous as never before had befal'n any Play" in his memory, or to blame the malice and prejudice of some spectators. He admitted that the Drury Lane company acted it well the first night "in most of its Parts" but on the second day, he asserts, "it was, for the most part, faintly and negligently Acted."[66]

In this season Drury Lane, in addition to Arsinoe, presented six brand new mainpieces, plus one revision and a new afterpiece, while there were three new mainpieces at the Haymarket and five at Lincoln's Inn Fields. The best known today are Colley Cibber's The Careless Husband, which played for nine consecutive nights, and Richard Steele's The Tender Husband, which played for five, but which did not draw well (although in subsequent seasons it did much better). Another new play presented at Drury Lane, The Quacks by Owen Swiney, adapted from Moliere's L'Amour Medecin, is worthy of a few lines of discussion because of the controversy it generated. Scheduled to make its debut at the Theatre Royal on March 22 as a benefit for the actor Ben Johnson, then languishing in prison, it was halted by the Lord Chamberlain. In the preface to the printed play, Swiney (he was called MacSwiney on the title page) states, "The Town were a little Surpriz'd, to find an Entertainment forbid upon the Day it was to be Represented; it seems . . . this Play was to be stiffl'd because the other House were to Act one upon the same Subject!"[67] Rich himself complained in a latter to the Lord Chamberlain that Swiney's play had been stopped and there was "... no Just reason for stopping it but kindness to Mr Vanbrugh."[68] However, the real reason for the stoppage was not Vanbrugh's influence, according to Albert Rosenberg, but rather the play's satirical attacks on Jacob Tonson and the Kit-Kat Club, of which Tonson was secretary.[69] When the offending material was removed, The Quacks was acted a week later, on March 29, and again on April 9 and 10. The play at the Haymarket was The Consultation, presented first on April 24.

The 1705-06 season is a rich one in two senses: there is much more information about various aspects of the theatre and Rich's dealings than in previous seasons. And Rich's company dominated the London stage operatically and financially (at this time there is a causal relationship between the two). It did not, as we shall see, do as well dramatically.

Each company now had access to two theatres: Rich's to Dorset Garden and Drury Lane, as it had in the past; Vanbrugh's (or Betterton's, if you prefer) to Lincoln's Inn Fields and the Haymarket. Most of the performances, however, were at Drury Lane and the Haymarket, to which Betterton et al moved after playing at Lincoln's Inn Fields until October 20. Ten days later they opened with a fine new comedy by Vanbrugh, who still owned the license which permitted Betterton's company to act. The play was The Confederacy, which despite (or perhaps because of) criticism that "it wanted just Decorum,"[70] gave four successive performances and ten in all during the season. Both in drawing power and quality it far surpassed the new play that Rich staged on the night of The Confederacy's premiere: Hampstead Heath by Thomas Baker, which endured only long enough to permit Baker his third night proceeds. Other plays by Vanbrugh were also presented: The Provoked Wife, somewhat altered, was given five times; The Mistake, which made its debut this season, held on for six consecutive nights plus one later performance; Squire Trelooby, in which he, Congreve and Walsh had a hand, received a new last act and was offered six times. Thus, Vanbrugh's own pieces played at least 28 nights. The reason for Vanbrugh's frenzied activity--but we should remember that Vanbrugh often did not create entirely new comedies but rather adapted a number of Moliere's--was that the playhouse of which he was so proud was losing its battle with Drury Lane. Congreve, who eight months ago had resigned from the management of the Queen's which he at first had shared with Vanbrugh, wrote to a friend on April 30, "I believe the playhouse cannot go on another winter. I have learned there is to be a union of the two houses as well as kingdoms."[71] Even Drury Lane joined the Vanbrugh bandwagon, staging his play The Pilgrim twice. In all, nine new entertainments were presented at the Haymarket to only six by Drury Lane. Of course, not all the performances were well done:

an unidentified young lady who wrote The Faithful General (Haymarket, January 3, 1706) stated in the preface to the play that it had been "deform'd and mangl'd" by Vanbrugh's company. The only other new play of note staged by the Haymarket was Nicholas Rowe's Ulysses, which was quite successful with an initial run of seven nights and four later performances, but by itself it could do little to moderate Vanbrugh's financial distress. Drury Lane presented no good new play; certainly Colley Cibber's Perolla and Izadora, which managed six nights, had little distinction. Its chief dramatic offering was The Recruiting Officer, Farquhar's popular comedy, which was given nine times.

This was the season when the attractiveness of opera became crystal clear. Rich presented operas on at least 39 nights (following The London Stage's listings, which don't always agree with contemporary counts), about one fourth of all performances (there were about 125 dramatic evenings at Drury Lane). Vanbrugh's repertory included about 12% opera, or roughly one evening in eight. There were three new operas at the Haymarket: The Temple of Love by Pierre Motteux, which endured for two nights;[72] The British Enchanters by George Granville (Lord Lansdowne), which was "very Exquisitly done, especially the Singing Part," and was repeated eight times; and a comical opera, Wonders in the Sun, by Thomas D'Urfey, whose five or six performances did not pay half its cost.[73] Rich presented last season's Arsinoe sixteen times, always preceded by some scenes from other plays. He also brought back Motteux' The Island Princess for eleven performances (it had last played in January, 1703), and tried John Dryden's King Arthur twice. Most important, on March 30 he introduced Camilla, with music by Bononcini and adaptation by Nicholini (often Niccoli) Haym, and the words Englished from the Italian by the useful Owen Swiney.

The contract which Haym signed with Rich is a particularly interesting one since it enables us to see how an opera in a foreign language was assembled for a Drury Lane production. The contract, signed January 14, 1706 (n.s.), shows that Haym had adapted both the instrumental and vocal music; the words were in Italian which Haym paid to have translated (by Swiney) into English prose. Rich then hired a Mr. Northman to change the English prose into English verse suitable to the score. Haym then wrote a new score to fit in with Northman's verse, making whatever changes were necessary. Haym, who had not completed the job at the time of the contract, agreed to work as quickly as he could to finish it. Also, Haym was to advise Rich in casting the parts, "to teach up the same parts and Musick" with diligence in his role as "Master Composer," to compose appropriate tunes for the dances, and to provide, at his own charge, two fair scores of the opera with the English words. Rich was to pay ₤100 to Haym, who promised not to perform in public any parts of the music either in its original Italian form, its recently altered English form, or as it might be altered by Motteux or anyone else, without Rich's approval. Among other details about the performance itself, we learn that Haym would play his own part on the bass viol.[74] Thus we can see how carefully Rich supervised the transition of Italian operas into English, and the foresight he demonstrated by providing for additional changes, if necessary, by Pierre Motteux (an experienced play and opera doctor, and the Lorenzo da Ponte of his time) or somebody else of Rich's own choosing. The Ь100 that Rich paid Haym was one of the best investments Rich ever made, _Camilla_ proving to be a vastly popular entertainment for many years.

Another document dating from this season, one which concerns an English opera singer of note, Catherine Tofts (it was her servant who in 1704 threw oranges and hisses at Signiora de l'Epine for tarnishing Mrs. Tofts' reputation), also discloses something about Rich's treatement of vocalists and about Rich himself.[75] In a tiff with Tofts, Rich apparently went to the Lord Chamberlain in very late 1705 or very early 1706 to force her to resume singing at Drury Lane. They had signed a contract providing for Tofts to sing for Rich for one year beginning January 5, 1705 (n.s.). During this year, according to her statement to the Lord Chamberlain, some members of the nobility gave her Ь60. Rich had the temerity to demand half of it. All those who listened to the arguments on both sides declared for Tofts, whereupon Rich revenged himself by scheduling her to sing more often than her health permitted, sometimes thrice in one week (possibly the week beginning June 11), not because Rich hoped to attract large crowds--since it was very hot and most people had fled London--but because of ill will. On the Tuesday of the following week she had lost her voice and thus could not sing. As a result Rich docked her Ь20 of the Ь100 she was to receive at the end of the season, and refused to restore it until she had sung twice. This she did. When she was to perform again at the beginning of this season (1705-06), she asked for new clothes, since her old ones were worn out and indeed had never been made fit for her. Rich answered, Tofts asserts, "that he supposed She had a mind to improve herself that she might be in a Condition to Raise her price." After enumerating several other complaints, she declares Rich is "a Man unfitt to deale with for his ill Manners & Management of them which are in his power." Tofts then offers several proposals for a new contract, among them that Rich give her Ь100 and release her from all forfeitures; that she receive Ь200 for 12 performances; that she be permitted to make up any performance that illness might cause her to miss; that she should have the Practicing Room to dress in, and two women to serve as dressers; that Rich provide her with two bottles of wine whenever she sang for the use of the gentlemen that practice with her; that she have a benefit on the following Tuesday, February

19; and finally, that after the contract ends and if Rich and she can't agree on the terms of a new one, she shall be able to sing where she wishes.[76] I do not know how Rich responded to her justification for her refusal to sing, or what reasons he adduced to justify his behavior, but Mrs. Tofts was with him in the following season. To us it certainly seems Rich had no right to demand half of the money members of the nobility gave her, and that he was particularly vindictive in his insistence that she sing what seems to her to be too freqently (i.e., three times in one week). But before passing any definitive judgment on Rich's behavior, which on the surface appears to be culpable, I think we ought to have his defense. As it stands, however, Mrs. Tofts' statements place Rich in a very bad light.

But it would be a mistake to think that relations between the managers and the actors in the rival company were always harmonious. Remember George Powell, former rehearsal director for Rich, who had been supplanted by Wilks and had been granted a discharge on April 7, 1705, and had joined Betterton's troupe? Powell, it developed, was not happy there, refused to obey orders, and only a few months into the season (on November 9) the Lord Chamberlain ordered that he be arrested. Ten days later Rich was commanded by the Lord Chamberlain not to accept Powell back because of his recalcitrant conduct at the Haymarket.

Powell was one of those players whose name was mentioned in a complaint lodged by Rich with the Lord Chamberlain on December 9, 1705, against Vanbrugh and Congreve (at that time he shared in the management), for seducing away Drury Lane performers. The specific actress whose departure served as the basis for Rich's complaint was Mary Hooke, alias Harcourt, who had been engaged by the Haymarket even though she signed five year articles with Rich in October, 1702. Rich accompanied his protest with a copy of a November 27, 1704 letter written by Sir John Stanley, the Lord Chamberlain's secretary, warning Rich not to engage any Lincoln's Inn Fields performers.[77] The implication, of course, is that what applies to Drury Lane should apply to the rival company. Rich also noted in his complaint that the effort to attract personnel attached to Drury Lane was far from unique: a prompter, Newman, and a dresser, Hood, had been tempted, and since Christmas seven Drury Lane players--Powell, Bowen, Doggett, Mins, Husbands, Mrs. Bignall and Mrs. Baker--had been engaged by Vanbrugh. The fact that Powell is cited suggests that Rich is lumping together those who left with permission and those who left without. One might ask why Rich should protest at this time about the departure of an actress who was not an important member of his troupe when he seems not to have done so earlier--three of those performers he names had left in the spring, two during the summer. Professor Milhous (Thomas Betterton, p. 204) explains that Rich did not

58

consider the Haymarket a genuine threat to his theatre's prosperity the previous season. Now apparently he did.

In the summer of 1706, his negotiations for a merger with Rich's company having been unsuccessful, Vanbrugh tried another tack--whether it was his own idea or someone else's I do not know. Realizing that the time was not yet ripe for a union with Rich, one which would compensate him very well, Vanbrugh attempted to have Owen Swiney take over the management of his company. Why Swiney? Ever since 1702 or 1703 he had been winning his way into Rich's trust, and had been performing more and more services for him. It is certain that Rich knew of Vanbrugh's offer, and it is probable that either directly or indirectly he suggested Swiney as a likely person to replace Vanbrugh. Rich himself seems to have sent for Swiney, who, like most upper-class Londoners, was out of town during the hot summer, to come to London. Vanbrugh then proposed to Swiney that he become the manager of the Haymarket, make whatever salary arrangement he could with the actors, take over the clothes and scenes and the theatre itself, as well as the license which Vanbrugh had received from Queen Anne only about twenty months ago. All Swiney had to do was to pay Ŀ5 a day theatre rent for every acting day; the total, however, was not to exceed Ŀ700 per year. Swiney asked for time to consider the proposal for a little while and to discuss it with Rich. Rich approved of the idea because he thought he could control Swiney, who owed him Ŀ200 (the debt, of course, would tend to make Swiney more pliable), and thus he could realize his ambition to direct the two legitimate theatres in London, although his control over one of them had to be kept secret. Quite a coup for him! To encourage Swiney to accept, and also (it would seem) to make clearer the difference between the appeal of plays on the one hand, and opera and other extra-dramatic entertainment on the other, he privately told Swiney to take whatever Drury Lane actors chose to move to the Haymarket, except Cibber. With this kind of understanding, then, on August 14, 1706 Swiney agreed to assume the direction of the Haymarket at Ŀ5 per acting day for the seven years remaining on Vanbrugh's lease. All this is how Cibber tells the story. (Apology, pp. 177-79) Unfortunately, it does not jibe in every detail with a letter to Cibber by Swiney himself on Saturday night, October 5, 1706, a letter so interesting and revealing that I shall print a large part of it. The letter tells us about some of Rich's questionable financial practices, which is nothing new. It tells us something about how the subscription for Camilla was organized. It tells us that Rich was given to using bad language and that he had much business with people who could be reached at White's Chocolate House and with people of the nobility or soon to join that patrician group. And, of course, it tells us much about Swiney's role.

Dear Colley

I undertook the management of the playhouse in the Haymarkett by and with the advice of some who were Mr Rich's
best friends but incensed against him because he trifled with
'em about Vanbrugh's businesse, he never really intending any
thing (but the gaining of time) by the treaty, his old play.
Well Whats that to me youl say--why I'll tell theee puppy.
Know then that Rich was to make a union of the houses and I
was to manage under him My Angel at 100 Guineas per annum
Salary & I was to have a place at court and the Devel and all
you know, upon this I quitted my post in the Army. In about
a fortnights time after this I found that Mr Rich intended
nothing but the going on his old way of paying Singers and
dancers and not paying the Actors. I did not think it was my
Interest to be Concerned on the wrong side, since I had no
obligation to stay with Mr Rich, he discharging me of my
promise the minute he broke of with Vanbrugh. Further my
Angel I thought if I had reason to complain now I was not in
his power I thought it wou'd be too late to seek redresse
when ever I shou'd be so unlucky as to fall into his hands
for you must know my Dear that Rich is as tyrannycall as
Lewis Le Grand, and I have as many grievances to complainn
off as Prince Ragotzki, [Francis Rakoczy II, Prince of Hun-
gary, who had been deceived by Louis XIV] I thought the best
way of doing my selfe right was to take up Arms and declare
for the liberty of the Actors who were oppressed by Singers
and dancers (Jesuits of a play house). And I think I shall
be as successfull as my Brother Princes who turn out another
upon the pretence of Mal administration and secure themselves
a greater power. But to be serious I will Exhibit a few
Articles against my Late Soveraign viz.

1. He sent for me from my Quarters in the North, I was
at a great charge in coming to town and you know it cost me a
great deal of mony last winter, I served him night and day,
nay all night and all day, for Nine Months. He sent me forty
pounds by Jack Hall as a return for my vast services, I bid
him carry back the mony to his Master with a bill of Jobs or
porterage to whites Chocolate house, Lord Whartons, Mr
Manwarings, & Mr Boyles, which at 2d a jobb came to above Ь50
13 s and 4d.

2. It was impossible for him to have the Opera of Camilla without me, he told me if I coud get a Subscription he
woud give me Ь100 50. to be disposed off to a gentleman that
was concern'd in the writing it, the other for the Industri-
ous Mr Siny. I applyd to Lord Wharton and his Grace of Rich-
mond, the Subscription was gott and Rich told me in the
Winter he woud let me have a part of a benefit from the

performance of it one day, he not being in a Condition to keep his word with me tho´ he received 1400. Guineas for it besides the Gallerys that time that the subscription was got by my Lord Wharton was for the Scotch nobility. Item for a great parcell of Ill language at several times and places, but that I think he never got the better of me at Except when Collonel Brett was by. Successe will determine who is in the right.

I did design to have communicated this matter to you as soon as you came from Windsor and was with Mr Wilks at your house the thursday friday Saturday Sunday & Monday before the businesse was discovered. It was to have been kept Secret a fortnight longer till I had gott the people I had pitcht upon among whom was Mr Cibber among the Betterton´s Wilk´s Barry´s &c the paper delivered to My Lord Chamberlain will be my Voucher, his Lordship was big of the plot and was afraid if any body shou´d let it be known at Court before him, he shou´d be Robbed of the glory of Establishing the Stage upon a foot of going on, he told it at the Dutchesse of Malbro´s the same day Wilks & Oldfield signed and if I had not been pretty brisk the whole matter might have miscarried, for on Monday Mills Bullock Keen Newman & Norris Signed, so that you may see I had no such mean design of lowering the Actors or starving ´em into a compliance with me, I am satisfied that it can´t be worse with the Actors any where than where they were as to their Salary, And to show you that I have a very great regard for Mr Cibber he shall be welcome to me when he sees which side is strongest tho´ it shou´d be ours. Estcourt must be had tho´ he has addrest Mr Rich. . . . Mr Rich might have had the house for Ł3 or Ł3 10s a day. I have taken a lease for 7: yeares at Ł5 per day. . . . I have given every Actor greater Salarys than Rich did and most of ´em benefits paying [MS reads "playing"] Ł40 charge. . . .[78]

The switch from Vanbrugh to Swiney was thus recorded by John Downes at the very end of his Roscius Anglicanus (p. 50):

. . . Captain Vantbrugg by Agreement with Mr. Swinny, and by the Concurrence of my Lord Chamberlain, Transferr´d and Invested his License and Government of the Theatre to Mr. Swinny; who brought with him from Mr. Rich, Mr. Wilks, Mr. Cyber, Mr. Mills, Mr. Johnson, Mr. Keene, Mr. Norris, Mr. Fairbank, Mrs. Oldfield, and other; United them to the Old Company . . .

And he refers twice to this event as a "Union," a questionable term. Congreve in a letter he wrote on September 10 more accurately describes it as a "revolution":

The play-houses have undergone another revolution; and
Swinny, with Wilks, Mrs Oldfield, Pinkethman, Bullock,
and Dicky [probably Norris], are come over to the Hay-
Market. Vanbrugh resigns his authority to Swinny,
which occasioned the revolt. Mr Rich complains and
rails like Volpone when counterplotted by Mosca. My
Lord Chamberlain approves and ratifies the desertion;
and the design is, to have plays only at the Haymarket, and operas only at Covent Garden [that is,
Drury Lane]. I think the design right to restore acting; but the houses are misapplied, which time may
change.[79]

There were two basic reasons, real or pretended, for Rich's complaining and railing. One was that Drury Lane would be restricted
to opera, a restriction which did not seem to bother some other
patentees, who thought that opera was much more profitable than
drama and without a group of actors to deal with, Rich's bookkeep-
ing would be simplified and it would be more difficult for him to
conceal the profits from them. Some of these ideas, and one or
two others, are advanced by Vanbrugh in a letter he wrote to the
Lord Chamberlain, probably in August of 1706, attempting to justify taking away from Rich the right to present plays:

> If any body shou'd endeavour to possess the Queen That
> the Persons concern'd in the Patent (besides Mr Rich) wou'd
> be prejudic'd by an establishment That shou'd confine acting
> to one house, and musick to tother. It is so evidently oth-
> erwise That 'tis the only means left to Restore 'em to any
> advantage, for the money they have in that adventure; as will
> beyond all Contest appear when it is observ'd.
>
> That in twelve years past, That Mr Rich has had the
> management in his hands. (tho' 'tis notorious he has spent
> Vast sums himself) he has not divided to those concern'd with
> him, one single shilling.
>
> That he own'd last year, he lost by his Players, what he
> got by his Opera; and by Consequence, his desire of keeping
> 'em on, can be for nothing, but to confound and embroil the
> Accounts and give him a Pretence to make no Dividend
>
> That is he has the Opera single & Entire The Profit must
> be so Certain, and the accounts will ly in so short and plain
> a Compass; That twill be impossible for him to deceive the
> People any Longer who have Claims to a share with him
>
> Whereas; if he go's on, in this Confus'd jumble, of a
> Double Company, There is no manner of Reason to believe,

They'll fare any better for twelve years to Come, Than they
have done for twelve years Past.

Memorandum
   To put Mr Riches design of Cheating the rest of the adventurers out of all question: There was an offer made him in
   August was twelve month, to put the Whole thing into his
   hands, and He refus'd it. owning very frankly that 'twas
   better for him to have it as 'twas to himself; than by res-
   toring the Patent to its former Condition to let in the Others to govern & share with him. This may be prov'd upon
   Oath.[80]

Was Rich himself only publicly angry but privately happy? At this
time he probably thought he still owned the services of Cibber,
who was in Gloucestershire at the home of a good friend, Colonel
Henry Brett, writing a play and unaware of the theatrical changes
occurring in London. When Cibber came to town in October--the
season was about a month late in starting due, probably, to the
unsettled conditions in both companies and to certain physical
"improvements" Rich had made in Drury Lane--he went to see Rich to
sign a contract for the coming season. By mail (in a letter
already printed), Cibber reveals, Swiney had attempted to induce
him to join the Haymarket company, but Cibber had deemed it wiser
to remain with Rich. But when Cibber learned so many of Rich's
actors had deserted that there were hardly enough to stage a play,
he asked Rich where the actors had gone and what he planned to do.
"Don't trouble yourself, come along, and I'll shew you," he
replied. Now let Cibber tell the story:

   He then led me about all the By-places in the House,
   and shew'd me fifty little Back-doors, dark Closets,
   and narrow Passages, in Alterations and Contrivances of
   which kind he had busied his Head, most part of the
   Vacation; for he was scarce ever, without some notable
   Joyner, or a Bricklayer extraordinary, in pay, for
   twenty Years. And there are so many odd obscure Places
   about a Theatre, that his Genius in Nook-building was
   never out of Employment; nor could the most vain-headed
   Author, be more deaf to an Interruption in reciting his
   Works, than our wise Master was, while entertaining me
   with the Improvements he had made in his invisible
   Architecture; all which, without thinking any one Part
   of it necessary; tho' I seem'd to approve, I could not
   help, now and then, breaking in, upon his Delight, with
   the impertinent Question of-- ᴮut, Master, where are
   your Actors? But it seems I had ᴄaken a wrong time for
   this sort of Enquiry; his Head was full of Matters of
   more moment. . . . (Apology, pp. 179-80)

63

Cibber explains Rich's disregard of the need for actors by his "notion . . . that Singing, and Dancing, or any sort of Exotick Entertainments, would make an ordinary Company of Actors too hard, for the best Set, who had only plain Plays to subsist on." (Apology, p. 180) This judgment, which I have quoted earlier, was an accurate and important one.

Cibber, who was quite understandably concerned about his salary since the absence of many of the actors would lead to empty houses, asked that Rich increase his pay for the coming season, or guarantee that he (Cibber) would receive the same amount of money he had received last season for as many days of acting. Rich refused to do either but instead offered him any parts previously belonging to the actors who had left Drury Lane. Cibber told him what terms he demanded and departed. Shortly afterwards--still following Cibber's account--Swiney came to Rich to ask him to sign a contract which was yet only verbal. Swiney, whose company had begun performing on October 14, was encouraged by the relative success of his plays, presented, as he advertised, "Without Singing or Dancing" in the entr-actes, repeated their agreement: Swiney should take the Hay-Market House in his own name, have what actors he thought necessary from Drury Lane, and after all obligations had been met, the profits should be equally divided between them. I have italicized the last clause to stress its significance: if Rich were not to control the second house outright, at least he would enjoy 50% of its profits. But Rich hesitated-- "Rashness was a Fault, that had never yet been imputed to the Patentee," says Cibber. (Apology, p. 181) Swiney wanted to know exactly what rights he did have and insisted that Cibber, if he was willing, should join his company. This Rich adamantly refused. The two argued, came to a rupture, and Cibber, when he discovered that Rich slighted him because he was certain that Swiney would not dare sign him, agreed to become a member of Swiney's company. (Apology, p. 181) According to one of Cibber's more recent and most painstaking biographers, so did Norris, Bullock and Johnson--after Cibber left, not before, as some others think.[80] Nine days after the Haymarket's company opened the 1706-07 season, Rich and his decimated company opened theirs at Dorset Garden, presumably because Rich's architectural changes had not yet been completed at Drury Lane. Note that I call Rich's company "decimated." Rich himself advertised his players as the "deserted Company of Comedians of the Theatre Royal" in the Daily Courant of October 23, 1706. Why did Rich wish to call attention to the pitiful condition of his troupe? Did he think it would arouse sympathy for his company? Did he think playgoers would be induced to attend a theatre whose complement of actors was so badly under-manned and under-womanned? Is there another explanation? I think there must be but it eludes me.

64

How successful were the two companies in 1706-07? We must remember that although no specific document has been found which states that the Haymarket was limited to strictly dramatic fare—no opera, not even singing or dancing between the acts—and that Rich could present any kind of entertainment (the loss he suffered was in performers, not in choice of repertoire), such seems to have been the case. Despite that restriction, Swiney seems to have done reasonably well. According to Cibber, plays recovered a good deal of their previous esteem, Swiney was "a considerable Gainer," he was able to discharge his Ŀ200 debt to Rich, and the salaries of some of the actors were "handsomely advanc'd" and regularly paid. (Apology, pp. 182, 184) Vanbrugh supports Cibber's evaluation. He wrote a letter in the spring of 1708 stating that Swiney had "a good deal of money in his Pocket; that he got before by the Acting Company."[82] With the assistance of Lord Halifax, a benefactor of the stage, a public subscription for reviving three plays of the best authors (i.e., Shakespeare, Fletcher, Dryden) with the full strength of the Haymarket company—each subscriber to have three tickets for the first day of each play for three guineas—was undertaken and caried out very successfully. But being forbidden any musical or dancing enhancement was a severe handicap. For example, The British Enchanters, by George Granville, Lord Lansdowne, had been presented twelve times the previous season but when Swiney attempted to stage it on December 10 minus those extras, Granville asked the Lord Chamberlain's office to halt the performance because singing and dancing were an essential part of it and Swiney's plan was "no other than a design to murder the Child of my Brain."[83] On the other hand, Rich publicized the fact that his programs included singing and dancing, and he produced several operas, two of which were extremely popular. One, Camilla, held over from the previous season, was given twenty times. Evidence of its popularity can be found in the preface to Mrs. Manley's tragedy Almyna, which opened at the Haymarket on December 16 and closed the following night. Mrs. Manley praises Betterton for the "unwearied care" he gave the production, and she praises Swiney for spending so much for the clothes, but she says Almyna came at an unfortunate time, "The immediate week before Christmas between Devotion and Camilla." (Avery, p. 135) Another opera, Thomyris, Queen of Scythia, despite its late debut (April 1) was repeated seven more nights and was greeted with as much encouragement "as would have furnished the town for a whole winter with as good tragedies and comedies as they have seen these twenty years."[84]

Let us stop for a moment to investigate Thomyris, because thanks to Vice Chamberlain Coke's papers we can learn much about the haggling that London theatre managers of the period (and, of course, their employees as well) were forced to undergo. Thomyris, although Jean Christophe Pepusch seems to have composed the recitatives, and Pierre Motteux to have furnished the story and the English words to fit the tunes,[85] is usually attributed to J.J. Heidegger, who arranged the music from Scarlatti and Bononcini. Certainly there were so many collaborators and so little original work by Heidegger that one might question how much credit and compensation Heidegger should receive, yet in his dealings with Rich it is clear that Heidegger regarded Thomyris as his own creation. Sometime in January, 1707, Rich wrote to the Lord Chamberlain, stating that 400 persons had subscribed 200 guineas for each of six performances of the opera and that he wanted to present it at Drury Lane "by the best Singers & Masters & well dress't designing to please the quallity in all things as well as he can . . . ."[86] Seeking to avoid "all differences" with Heidegger, Rich proposed that Heidegger nominate two of the noble subscribers and Rich would nominate two others. The four would determine how the subscription money should be divided between the two. If the four couldn't decide, then they would nominate an "Umpire" to make the final decision. Then Rich made another proposal: he was willing "in order to make the Translation of this Medley Opera his own with the Score & parts To lay out 300d Guineas in the Dressing & Decoration of it & for Printed Books for the Subscribers [i.e., libretti]" and Heidegger would have all the subscription money for the fourth and sixth days, a total of 400d Guineas, and Rich would have the rest of the money. Were Heidegger to agree to this, he (Heidegger) would deliver the score and parts as soon as they were finished--at the time of the letter much of the third act had not been completed nor had the part of Orontes been altered for Valentini, who was to sing it. Rich mentions that he paid less than ₤200 for the translation and score of Camilla and less than ₤200 for another opera as good as Camilla, and thus Rich is giving twice as much for Heidegger's opera, which, Rich notes, "he hath not a good Opinion of." Rich also points out that in the presence of the Lord Chamberlain and Lord Halifax he had "engag'd" to perform an opera written by Congreve and set to music by (John) Eccles (the opera, Semele, was doomed not to be performed until 1972) before Heidegger had offered Thomyris to him. Rich concludes by confessing that he "thinks himselfe hardly used to putt by other good Bargains meerly for Mr Heideggers Interest & profitt." A short time later, on January 17, Heidegger presented his own terms to the Lord Chamberlain: the entire receipts of the third and sixth days of performing Thomyris; the receipts on the 10th and 20th days less the charge of the house, in return for which Heidegger would give Rich the opera "with all the parts drawn out and renounce any further advantage."[87] Just what the payments actually were remains a mystery but certainly in this instance an unprejudiced observer might think that Heidegger was driving a very hard bargain indeed, especially for a work so heavily indebted to other hands than his own.

While not all Drury Lane operas were so successful--for example, _Rosamond_, which Addison wrote and for which Thomas Clayton provided the music, lasted only three nights--enough were to make the season profitable. Another factor to be considered in Drury Lane's income is that Rich's two new operas (they were the only new productions he offered this season) were supported by subscription, by which the front and side boxes were laid into the pit and admission to these areas was by subscription ticket only. The _Muses Mercury_ in December testified to opera's attractiveness: "The opera has been always crowded since it has been under the present management, and is now in a fairer way to live than ever."[88] Indeed, opera's appeal was such that Swiney felt moved to write to the Lord Chamberlain on January 27, complaining that he labored "under the disadvantage of Mr. Rich's being suffered to act plays, notwithstanding the extraordinary encouragement the town has given the opera."[89] The prosperity of one theatre does not necessarily dictate the poverty of the other, but sometimes there is a connection. Another obstacle that Swiney had to overcome was the wideness of the Haymarket which interfered with the acoustics there. Cibber mentioned that several of the new plays Swiney presented met with a much better reception when given at Drury Lane because of the "Difficulty of Hearing" at the Haymarket. (_Apology_, p. 182) Among those new plays--Swiney offered four mainpieces, plus two revisions and one afterpiece--by far the most successful was Farquhar's sparkling comedy _The Beaux' Stratagem_, which was staged on ten nights, not consecutively. The _Muses Mercury_ strikes another negative note about Swiney's company in the spring of 1707:

> Indeed 'tis necessary those who have served the stage
> should do their utmost to support her, for there's lit-
> tle hopes of her maintaining herself by the credit and
> character of her new servants. . . . We don't hear of
> any other play of note that will be represented this
> season, and cannot hope for many more the next, unless
> the poets are encouraged a little. . . ."[90]

A keen theatre historian, Professor Milhous, who has studied the period carefully, believes that both theatres did well in the 1706-07; the Haymarket "enjoyed real prosperity this season, and as far as one can judge, Rich had a decent year following a very different repertory policy."[91]

As we have seen, Rich had seemed quietly eager to let some of his best actors (not Cibber) move to the Haymarket, yet we know that Rich sued a number of actors, individually, for breaking their contracts. Why would he do so? Perhaps because Swiney's company had become stronger than he had envisioned; perhaps because he had quarreled with Swiney and wanted to harry him and his company. He instituted suit against both Cibber and Wilks for violating their 1704 articles by acting at the Haymarket and Wilks also for acting at Oxford in the summer. In addition, he sued Norris and Bullock on the same grounds and having won his case he persuaded them to put in writs of error. For these writs Swiney and Vanbrugh provided bail. Rich then told Norris and Bullock that he would not ask them for damages if they promised not to prosecute the writs. Once the two actors agreed, Rich then sued Vanbrugh and Swiney for the bail.[92] These legal actions, bordering on the unethical as they do, seem to justify Charles Gildon's terming Rich "a pettifogger in Law."[93]

It was also during this season that Rich introduced another innovation, financial, of course, not theatrical. He was credited with originating half-price, that is, allowing people into the theatre after the third act (the mainpiece almost always had five acts) upon payment of half the regular price. The unknown author of Three Original Letters states that Rich conceived of the idea to satisfy his murmuring office and door-keepers who were allowed to divide the after-money among themselves.[94]

The summer of 1706 had been full of incident for Christopher Rich. Two events occurred during the summer of 1707, one which led to the termination of Rich's management two years later. It was, in other words, the beginning of the end, although there was little hint of its dire effects from its innocuous beginnings. But first I want to deal with the other, much less significant. You will remember that Richard Steele's comedy, The Tender Husband, had premiered at Drury Lane in the 1704-05 season. During the following winter two performances of The Tender Husband were given, ostensibly for the author's benefit. When Steele did not receive the profits from these two benefits, he sued Rich; the bill was filed on July 3, 1707. Rich's response is full and detailed, and from it we learn that Rich did recognize Steele as a promising playwright, insisted that a friendship existed between him and Steele, and arranged to have Steele bring his next play to Drury Lane in exchange for a loan of ₤72.[95] The case reveals Rich as a hard but fair businessman whose knowledge of the facts is much greater than Steele's. The outcome of the case may have contributed to Steele's unflattering portrait of Rich as Devito in The Tatler.

Now for the other event, which began simply as a visit during the hot summer days of one friend with another: Sir Thomas Skipwith, the holder of either five-sixths or three-fifths of the patent, visited his intimate friend, Colonel Henry Brett at Brett's estate in Sandywell, Gloucestershire. As he had on a number of previous occasions, Skipwith grumbled to Brett that Rich had refused to provide any profit and loss accounting of his

68

management, that he (Skipwith) had received nothing from his share
of the patent for ten years, and he offered his rights in the
patent to Brett. They both laughed about what Skipwith had not
made of it and what Brett might do with it, and agreed that Brett
would purchase Skipwith's share of the patent for the token sum of
ten shilings. The deed, prepared by an attorney who also was
Brett's house guest, was signed on October 6, 1707. When Brett
came to London, he acquainted Cibber with his new "Theatrical
Power," and asked his advice how best to proceed, even though
Cibber was now a member of the Haymarket company. Cibber, who had
heard the chimes at midnight with Brett, urged him to waste no
time and to demand that he share with Rich "all Effects, and
Powers" to which the deed entitled him. Cibber told Brett to be
forceful, and to "give himself the air at least, of Enquiry into
what had been done, so that what he intended to be might be
thought more considerable, and be the readier comply'd with." He
warned Brett that he should not allow Rich ever to seem wiser than
himself; if he did, then Rich would perplex him "with absurd and
dilatory measures." In a very revealing judgment, Cibber observed
that Rich could not deal directly and plain because of "his
natural Diffidence." As evidence, Cibber cited Rich's reneging on
the verbal agreement he had with Swiney about their joint use of
the Haymarket. And Cibber gave it as his opinion that although
"some People thought it Depth, and Policy in him, to keep things
often in Confusion. . . they over-rated his Skill, and that in
reality his Parts were too weak, for his Post, in which he had
always acted, to the best of his Knowledge." (This is another
important evaluation, somewhat questionable, I think; I shall consider it later.) Cibber reminded Brett of Sir Thomas Skipwith, who
had trusted too much to Rich's capacity "for this sort of Business" and as a result never received any profits from it. If,
Cibber told Brett, he were firm he could lead "this, hitherto
untractable Menager" into whatever channel he (Brett) wanted to
direct it. In Cibber's mind the only scheme which would raise the
patent to its former value was to unite the two companies, and
Rich would not willingly consent to that--"this close Menager
would secretly lay all possible Rubs in the way. . . ." But there
was a way to do that, Cibber felt. Though Rich's caution "would
never part with a Straw, by way of Concession, yet to a high Hand,
he would give up any thing, provided he was suffer'd to keep his
Title to it: If his Hat were taken from his Head, in the Street,
he would make no farther Resistance, than to say, I am not willing
to part with it." Cibber was sure Rich would not have the "Reso-
lution" to oppose any just measures advanced by someone with an
equal right to his and who was determined to carry them through.
Although Rich had a marked temper--something that both of them
were familiar with--Cibber told Brett that he could cope with it:
in dealing with so "exotick a Partner" it was advisable to use "a
good deal of Entertainment, and Humour" and by "softening the

Business, into a Diversion" the difficulties would be lessened.

Neither Cibber nor any one else seems to have recorded whether Brett dealt smoothly or vigorously with Rich, but that he succeeded in promptly bringing about what Cibber considered a desideratum (the uniting of the companies) is beyond question. We have to assume that Rich was shown the deed that transferred the patent right to Brett, that he was filled with dismay as Brett inserted himself into the affairs at Drury Lane without wasting any time, and that the dismay became alarm as Brett obtained the ear first of the Vice-Chamberlain, Thomas Coke, with whom he was intimately acquainted and through the Vice-Chamberlain the ear of the Lord Chamberlain. But if, as envisioned, Drury Lane were to be the exclusive home of drama, and the Haymarket the exclusive home of opera, how would Swiney feel, Swiney who had been placed at the head of the actors hardly more than a year ago? Swiney did not object, Cibber tells us, because opera was very popular indeed at this time.[96] In the second half of December (the timing in all probability is not coincidental) a number of complaints against Rich were filed with the Lord Chamberlain's office. First, Mrs. Tofts, no stranger to disharmony with Rich and a woman with a reputation for avarice,[97] wrote to the Vice Chamberlain, Thomas Coke, that a performance of the opera Thomyris could not have taken place "without having matters settled" had not Rich's friends prevailed upon the Lord Chamberlain. One may question her statement: Rich seems to have had very little influence with the Lord Chamberlain and there is evidence to suggest that the Lord Chamberlain strongly disliked him. In the letter Mrs. Tofts mentioned that she had laid out 80 guineas for clothes that she needed in Camilla "by ye order of a Noble man who is Mr Riches best friend with Mr Rich's consent." I wish we could discover whether this was true and just who this noble friend of Rich was. A week or so later, probably, the father of a singer who had left Rich the previous month, Littleton Ramondon, complained that his son had not been paid.[98] A third group of complaints, bearing the date December 31, 1707, and written by a musician, Charles Dieupart, charged Rich with failing to observe the terms of his agreements with fourteen singers, dancers and orchestra members.[99] Margaritta (so spelled by Dieupart but more commonly Margherita; her last name is de l'Epine) wanted twenty guineas for singing twice in the opera the previous season. Mrs. Tofts, via Dieupart, continued her pursuit of the eight guineas for the clothes she wore in Camilla and made several interesting points. She states that it was unreasonable for her to lose his sum because "the cloaths that were made by Mr Rich for Camilla" were paid for by the nobility and were used in Rosamond (the Addison-Clayton opera that failed) and "paid for again out of the subscription money" from Rosamond. In other words, Mrs. Tofts was claiming that Rich himself did not lay out any money for the opera clothes, but that

subscriptions paid for the clothes--twice. I have not been able
to prove or disprove the allegation. She went on to assert that
Rich "cannot say that he ever made more than 3 suits of cloaths"
for her although she performed in four operas--Arsinoe, Camilla,
Rosamond, and Thomyris--"every one of the said operas having been
subscrib'd for, and money allow'd for cloaths & and sceans. &c."
She stressed that because she played the principal roles she had
"to be at very great Expences for several things that the house
never allow's for, as Locks for hair, jewells, ribbons for knotts
for the head & body, muslin for vails, gloves, shoes, washing of
vails and head cloaths, and many more things, for which she may
modestly afirm that one hundred pounds is not sufficient for the
season." Littleton Ramondon, whose father had filed a petition
(at least partially unjustified) on his son's behalf just about a
week earlier, now complained again that Rich refused to pay him
upon Ramondon's signing with the Haymarket. Three dancers (Char-
lier, Debargues and Mlle Debargues) did not come to an agreement
with Rich because they chose to desert to the Haymarket and they
wanted to be reimbursed for their expenses. Additionally, eight
musicians, Dieupart among them, "who were turn'd out of Drury Lane
Play house by Mr Rich upon suspicion of being concern'd in the
Project of Acting Opera's in the Haymarkett" (understandable
behavior on Rich's part, surely) wanted to be paid the same amount
at the Haymarket as they would have received from Rich, although
they would be working much longer and harder at the Haymarket.
They suggested that in the event Rich were to be limited in the
frequency of his presentations of plays or operas (The Lord
Chamberlain's order of union, dated the same day Dieupart's complaint was obviously unknown to him) they should receive more
money for each performance. Dieupart concluded by urging some
consideration be given to Heidegger "who has laid out a Considerable summe of money. . . ."

    While negotiations were being carried on, Rich and his
manager at the time, Richard Estcourt, were asked to attend at
least one meeting with the Lord Chamberlain or his surrogate. On
December 30, 1707, we know that the two were told to be present at
a 11:00 A.M. meeting on Tuesday, December 30 at which, in all probability, the final terms of the union were to be discussed.[100]
Estcourt, pleading rheumatic fever, did not attend. On the following day, December 31, the Lord Chamberlain issued the order
which united the companies as of January 10, 1708 (n.s.). The
order stressed that the players were suffering because of the
division of the companies and could not gain "a reasonable sub-
sistence," that the plays could not be acted to their best advantage, and that the charges of maintaining a company of comedians
and opera performers in the same company were too great to be
borne. All operas and other musical performances were to be given
at the Queen's (i.e., the Haymarket). The company at Drury Lane

and Dorset Garden could receive actors from any other playhouse, but they were strictly forbidden to perform any musical entertainments, nor could they receive any dancers or other performers in music other than instrumental music.[101] This order, as Professors Milhous and Hume point out in their valuable article, "The Silencing of Drury Lane in 1709,"[102] was both "unprecedented" and "of dubious legality." Rich, as the chief patentee (in terms of actual control of the Drury Lane company, not in the percentage of the patent he controlled, only 1/6) must have known that the terms of the patent allowed him to perform all kinds of entertainments, but he probably knew that the Lord Chamberlain was strongly prejudiced against him and would be unlikely to alter his ruling unless Rich would resort to a lengthy process of law. As his involvement in many law suits would indicate, Rich was not averse to litigation, but he knew that the Lord Chamberlain, an officer of the Queen, was a very powerful opponent, and as Rich possibly did not know, an opponent determined not to yield. A manuscript in the Harvard Theatre Collection (Coke #76) reveals that Kent's secretary, Sir John Stanley, wrote to Vice Chamberlain Coke that he (Stanley) had "taken all possible care to prevent their playing to day" after receiving a letter from the Lord Chamberlain in which, Stanley stated, "I find him resolv'd to hold it out to ye last." And there was a brighter side, too: Rich would now have a monopoly on drama, something he had lost in 1695 when Lincoln's Inn Fields was licensed. And as a monopolist, he would be in an enviable position to deal with actors and determine their salaries. All things considered, the Lord Chamberlain's edict could have been worse. There was a general influx and exodus, the actors at the Haymarket joining the relatively few at Drury Lane, and the singers and dancers at Drury Lane moving to the Haymarket. Only ten days after the union Vanbrugh was explaining two of his problems to the Vice Chamberlain. One concerned the high salaries singers and musicians were demanding which made it "impossible" to complete the season unless the performers were "reduc'd to Reason."[103] The other problem is of more interest to us because Vanbrugh suggested that Rich was secretly attempting to undermine the Haymarket:

> There will be an other misfortune, a Great one if not nip'd in the Bud. I mean musick meetings. There's one given out to morrow at York Buildings, and the Bills larger & much more remarkable than usuall. I'm told, (and believe) Rich is in the Bottom on't. But I hope you'll move My Lord Chamberlain for an Order to stop their Performance. Which will be a great means to make our musitians both accept reasonable sallarys and be carefull in their Business.

I do not know whether Rich was "in the Bottom on't" but the

concert was postponed and it is quite likely that the Lord Chamberlain halted the performance in response to Vanbrugh's plea.

Upon uniting, Cibber says, both theatres immediately prospered. (Apology, p. 212) But is Cibber's memory to be relied on? It is certainly true that the Haymarket seems to have done well, because receipts for its fourteen opera performances from January 13 to March 8 averaged a very substantial Ⱡ135. However, although the proceeds from subscriptions and tickets sold at the box office were very high, so were the expenses. Vanbrugh, writing on May 14, 1708, about paying the singers and dancers at the Haymarket, says that he who is "so vast a sufferer by this years adventure" is "so hard run in this unhappy Business, that there is no room left for Generosity."[104] The prosperity that Cibber describes may have been experienced at Drury Lane: their proceeds certainly were much lower, but so were their expenses. But the prosperity certainly could not have been founded on the reception of Drury Lane's three new plays. Charles Goring's Irene lasted for only three performances (February 9, 10, 11); Lewis Theobald's The Persian Princess lasted only two (May 31, June 1); William Taverner's The Maid's The Mistress lasted only two (June 5, 7). Despite Cibber's waxing enthusiastic about the superlative performances the union guaranteed (Apology, p. 212), Irene was very poorly presented partly because it was deprived of music and partly because it was poorly acted. Wrote Goring in the preface to the printed Irene: "I am sensible . . . that IRENE appear'd to the greatest Disadvantage on the Stage, strip'd of Her Ornaments of Musick by a Superior Order; and in many of Her Characters suffering very much in the Action."[105]

What was happening on the Drury Lane stage during this season was in many ways less interesting than what was happening behind it: the power struggle between Rich and Brett. Despite the increased profits that Cibber says the playhouse enjoyed, Rich was not at all pleased

> to see his Power daily mould'ring from his own Hands, into those of Mr. Brett; whose Gentlemanly manner of making every one's Business easy to him threw their old Master under a Disregard, which he had not been us'd to, nor could with all his happy Change of Affairs, support. Although . . . [Rich] had acquitted [sic; acquired is probably intended] the Reputation of a most profound Politician, by being often incomprehensible, yet I am not sure, that his Conduct at this juncture, gave us not an evident Proof, that he was, like other frail Mortals, more a slave to his Passions, than his Interest; for no Creature ever seem'd more fond of Power, that so little knew how to use it, to his Profit

and Reputation; otherwise he could not possibly have been so discontented, in his secure, and prosperous State of the Theatre, as to resolve, at all Hazards, to destroy it. (Apology, pp. 212-13)

I am reluctant, without hard evidence, to accept Cibber's statement about Drury Lane's prosperity, but his understanding of Rich's character seems perceptive. Many human beings are loath to see control slip from their hands. Rich was one of them. Many human beings resent the intrusion of an interloper with no related business experience. Rich was one of them. Further, it is not all clear that if Brett were to be the dominant manager and all the theatre's profits were to be openly and honestly announced, and everyone who was entitled to any kind of compensation from Drury Lane received it, that the profits would be greater than they had actually but secretly been. It is possible that Rich's motivation to oppose Brett in any way he could was based not only on his desire for power but also for profit.

More than once Cibber tells us of Rich's chicanery dealing with the shareholders in the theatre building. To avoid paying their nightly share of the proceeds Rich deliberately tried to create "Confusion"--the term is Cibber's. For Rich confusion was preferable to orderliness because confusion was not really confusion to Rich but a secret state of order. There can be no doubt that those who had purchased shares in the theatre building were not paid regularly and were very much irritated (for some infuriated would be a better word) by Rich's methods. There were at least thirteen suits filed by shareholders who claimed that they had been deprived of their share of the theatre rent between 1694 and 1705 in which Rich was a co-defendant. He was also co-defendant in three suits asserting profits in the theatre had not been paid.[106] Rich himself had been trying to acquire a number of the 36 building shares of Drury Lane. Charles Killigrew, who held nine shares was the chief lessee, and there were 15 others who held from 3/5 of one share to four in 1695, the year after the first Sir Thomas Skipwith died.[107] Rich owned none at that time. But by March 1708 he had collected the two shares of May Scrope, one of Edward Watty, and the 3/5 share of Henry Hale (or Heiles).

Periodically Rich seems to have involved the shareholders in some theatrical matters when he chose to. One revealing case in which he did so concerned Thomas Phillips, a fruiter who had held the sole right to sell oranges, lemons and sweetmeats at Drury Lane since 1695. Originally he had paid ₤4 a week for the monopoly. Whether it was reduced upon the separation of the two theatres, and if so by how much, and whether Phillips had paid any arrears, was in dispute between him and the patentees. As the case is recorded, it seems that Rich was determined not to allow any fruiters -- limited to six in the contract -- into the pit, boxes and galleries during a play except during the playing of the music, and not at all when operas were given, except in the 18 penny gallery. After the Drury Lane company was split and the Haymarket opened (in April of 1705), Rich informed Phillips that there would be nothing but operas acted twice a week (a schedule Rich did not adhere to) "which would be worth nothing" to Phillips. He informed Phillips that if he felt any money was owing to him (Phillips) he should notify Charles Killigrew (the chief shareholder in the theatre) that the "Lessors or Builders owed him money on account of the Fruit," and further, that he (Rich) was planning to hire other persons to sell fruit and sweetmeats at Drury Lane. When Killigrew received the message, he suggested to Phillips that he send one or two people to try to sell fruit and sweeetmeats at the theatre. Phillips did try, but Rich "thrust them out."[108] While Phillips undoubtedly believed that he had been treated inconsiderately by Rich, it is quite possible that many of the theatre's patrons applauded Rich's effort to rid his theatre of untimely distractions or to control them more closely. But I would not want to state unequivocally that this was the sole reason for Rich's behavior in this case.

In general Rich had led the shareholders a "Chancery chase" but now he decided to try to win them over so that they would help him--or at least abstain from helping Brett--in his effort to harass the new patentee until he wearied of interfering in the management of Drury Lane. Cibber tells us that he proposed to make these shareholders "some small Dividend of the Profits (though he did not design that Jest should be repeated)" and to admit them to some share in the government of the theatre with the intention that they would always side with the now fair and just old manager. (Apology, p. 213) Since Brett owned either 3/5 or 5/6 of the patent, and Rich only 1/6, the most that the "minor patentees" of whom a Cibber biographer speaks (Barker, p. 75) could own would be only 7/30 of the patent. Therefore, Brett would be left in control. So it is difficult to comprehend how these minor patentees and/or the shareholders Rich was courting could swing the balance of power. Cibber, as in so many other instances, is not always clear. At any rate, following him with circumspection, we learn that Rich, in addition to gaining the support of the shareholders (sometimes called adventurers) also "took care that the Creditors of the Patent, who were, then, no inconsiderable Body, should carry off the every Weeks clear Profits, in proportion to their several Dues and Demands." (Apology, p. 213) His purpose, of course, was to demonstrate to Brett that the operation of a theatre company was not nearly so profitable as earlier seemed to be. Apparently Rich succeeded. After five or six months of running Drury Lane, Brett tired of fighting Rich and the clique of shareholders he had gathered around him, and perhaps the "minor patentees;" he had had enough of the wearying other tasks of playhouse management, whether or not the playhouse was prosperous, and on March 31, 1708, he abandoned Drury Lane and appointed three of the company's leading actors, Robert Wilks, Cibber (who was Brett's close friend) and Richard Estcourt, to assume the management.

But in the following season, 1708-09, it was Rich who directed Drury Lane, not Wilks, Cibber and Estcourt. Somehow he must have gained the power to control the theatre's affairs, perhaps through consolidating the building shareholders and the "minor patentees" behind him. It was a season filled with interesting and often unusual episodes, the last series of which was to result in the termination of Rich's management of the playhouse and his disassociation with the staging of plays and operas. As has been my practice, I shall first discuss the season as it was performed on the stages of the Haymarket--which was limited to producing Italian opera two nights a week, Tuesday or Wednesday and Saturday--and Drury Lane, which was restricted to the performance of plays on six nights a week. Rich's company began to act on August 26, but the Haymarket's opening was delayed. Despite the lack of competition, however, apparently Drury Lane did not do well. Richard Steele wrote in early October that "The taste for plays is expired. We are all for operas performed by eunuchs every way impotent to please."[109] The death of Queen Anne's husband, Prince George of Denmark, on October 28 prevented Swiney's company from initiating its season and also resulted in Drury Lane's closing. Both theatres were idle until December 14. Thus it is not difficult to understand why the first few months of the season were not propitious. Rich's company introduced five new plays, only one of which was successful, Susanna Centlivre's The Busie Body, which overcame an unpromising debut on May 12. The Queen's contented itself with one new opera, Clotilda, the music largely by Francesco Conti, presented on March 2. It died after seven performances in spite of the contribution made by the expensive scenery painted expressly by "two famous Italian Painters (lately arriv'd from Venice) and all the other Decorations." Swiney, however, advertised and used them in the frequent repetitions of Pyrrhus and Demetrius (Avery, p. 189). Rich's troupe presented a number of older, well-respected plays including several by Shakespeare and Jonson. A new play which Drury Lane staged on May 1, Thomas D'Urfey's The Modern Prophets, I cite not because of its popularity (it ran only three nights) but because in the preface to the printed version (1709) D'Urfey praises Rich: "The Kindness shewn by Mr. Rich in letting me be the first to raise the Prizes for my Benefit was not only advantageous to me, but a further

76

Encouragement to future Authors likewise. . . ." (p. 124)

Again this season some of the most interesting events were occurring off the stage rather than on. One of the most striking was the effort by Sir Thomas Skipwith to recover the patent rights he had so carelessly bestowed upon Brett on October 6, 1707. Whether Rich played any part in Skipwith's suit, urging him to file it so that Rich could have a co-patentee much less aggressive than Brett, I do not know, but it is certainly possible. The suit was filed on February 1, 1709 (n.s.) against Brett alleging that Skipwith had given the patent rights to Brett only on trust, that Brett had persuaded him it was not necessary to prepare any declaration of trust because if knowledge of it got out Brett's effectiveness would be lessened, and that he (Skipwith) "might safely rely" on Brett's "Fidelity and Integrity." Brett had also assured him that he (Brett) would later write a statement that the transfer of patent rights was only in trust, to be returned whenever Skipwith wished. In his bill of complaint (P.R.O. C8 481/66) Skipwith asserted that contrary to statements Brett made, there was no valuable consideration and no sum of money paid to him by Brett. Skipwith noted that Brett had received "very Considerable summs of Money" from the operation of Drury Lane, had refused to give Skipwith any accounting, and had allowed Skipwith "to be sued troubled or Molested" for the rent and other charges of the playhouse, and that a large amount of money was now being demanded of Skipwith on account of the rent, or the arrears in rent, without Brett's making any attempt to pay them.

Brett's detailed response to Skipwith's lengthy bill came on February 17. In it Brett insisted that Skipwith had told him that he (Skipwith) had received nothing from Drury Lane for 12 years and did, in fact, part "with considerable sumes of money under pretence of carrying the business of the said Play house," and was afraid that on account of his association with Drury Lane he would be "drawn in and subjected to Great Debts and demands." Brett denied unequivocally that any mention was made of the transfer being in trust, and advanced the idea that Skipwith's grant was motivated by his desire "to remove an Inconveniencie from himself and to bestow it" on Brett, Skipwith "being Jealous of Great charges debts and demands likely to pursue him Unlesse he parted therewith." Brett stated that since Skipwith in kindness had "freely and absolutely bestowed" the patent rights upon him, he (Brett) did plan to return them when the theatre was in "an Improved Condicon [sic]" but not because of any trust obligation. Brett asserts that he had concerned himself in the management of the playhouse, devoted much time and money to it, and has brought the theatre into a "better Posture and unto a considerable Improvem^t." Brett admits that he received "small summes of mony out of the said Play house or on account thereof," but that these

77

sums fall "very Short of reimbursing the charges he has been at . . . ." In a further answer (C10 545/39) about six months later (on July 29), Brett denies that he permitted Skipwith to be dunned for the theatre rent or any other charges, having directed Zachary Baggs, Drury Lane cashier, to pay all rents and charges incurred since the execution of the deed. If Skipwith is being hounded for money, it is because of debts incurred before Brett assumed the management.[110]

Cibber relates that Brett made no further defense of his cause. For this Cibber offers three reasons: Brett knew that everyone was aware he had paid nothing for the patent right; he was fearful that his keeping the patent rights might be misunderstood "and not favourably spoken of"; the profits, though large, were "constantly swallow'd up" by paying off old debts. Finally, Brett grew "so tir'd of the Plague, and Trouble, the whole Affair had given him," that he "withdrew himself, from all Concern with the Theatre and quietly left Sir Thomas to find his better Account in it."[111]

At the risk of complicating the chronology, let me briefly finish the Skipwith-Brett imbroglio. It was late in the summer of 1708 or a few months afterward that Sir Thomas was allowed "to find his better Account." Upon his death at Bath on June 5, 1710,[112] he was succeeded by his son, Sir George Bridges Skipwith. Then, after Brett was "allow'd the Charges he had been at, in his Attendance, and Prosecution of the Union," he yielded the share of the patent he had obtained from Sir Thomas to his heir, Sir George.

At the beginning of the season, on September 7, an advertisement appeared in the Daily Courant announcing the availability of the now deserted theatre in Lincoln's Inn Fields for use as a tennis court or for any other purpose other than that of a playhouse. Despite the caution that it could not be used as a playhouse, Rich was interested in the theatre--more than interested. And it was about this date--a few months before or a few months after--that Rich's name was first connected with the theatre which was to occupy his final days and which he was to bequeath to his two sons. The overseers' account books for St. Clement Danes (they are sometimes called the poor rates) carry the notation "Rich esq. nothing" for the period from May 14, 1708 to May 14, 1709.[113] This suggests that Rich was interested in the building but that he had not leased it yet, since he paid no taxes. In the previous year (May 14, 1707-08) no one's name appears in the rate books opposite the property, and for the year before 1706-07,[114] William Penkethman's name is written without assessment. Penkethman (spelled Pinckeman in the book) is, of course, the well-known comedian and minor theatrical impressario who was to control

78

the summer theatre at Greenwich in 1710. Rich's name was to disappear from the rate book for 1709-10 to be replaced by "Pinkeman." Cibber, who erroneously states that Rich "had taken a lease, at a low rent, ever since Betterton's company had first left it," wonders at Rich's concern for the old theatre:

> What are we to think of his taking this Lease, in the height of his Prosperity, when he could have no Occasion for it? Was he a Prophet? Could he then foresee, he should, one time or other, be turn'd out of Drury-Lane? Or did his mere Appetite of Architecture urge him to build a House, while he could not be sure, he should ever have leave to make use of it? (Apology, p. 232)

I cannot be sure what was in Rich's mind, but I can point out that he did not make any arrangements for leasing it until sometime between May 14, 1708 and May 14, 1709, during which period his management of Drury Lane was being contested by Wilks, Cibber and Estcourt, to whom Brett had given the patent. We should not forget that Rich was then operating Dorset Garden and that he must have been aware of the plans to tear it down; the actual destruction took place in late spring of 1709. The Daily Courant for June 1 records that "The Play-House at Dorset-Stairs is now pulling down." In a sense, then, Lincoln's Inn Fields was a potential replacement for Dorset Garden, Rich might have reasoned.

What served as a catalyst in bringing about an end to Rich's term of management at Drury Lane was his relations with his actors, which became increasingly strained this season. First, as Cibber related, many of the Drury Lane performers "were actually, if not injudiciously, reduc'd in their Pay, and others given to understand the same Fate was design'd them . . . ." (Apology, p. 215) Rich's next move was even more unpopular and threatening to the actors: he tried to reduce by one-third the money an actor took in on his benefit night. Since he so closely followed the financial operations of the theatre, Rich had observed that benefit nights were often extremely profitable to his performers, and, following Cibber, the benefit arrangements were very largely verbal. This is not to suggest that no benefits in this period were written into the articles of agreement. For example, Mrs. Barry seems to have had benefit provisions in her 1694 articles, and Doggett had definitely stipulated for a benefit in 1696.[115] Rich undoubtedly thought that there would be no problem since he was simply carrying out an agreement made the previous spring, on March 31, 1708, between Henry Brett (when he was in the possession of Skipwith's share of the patent) and the three actor managers, Wilks, Cibber, and Estcort. Effective June 10, 1708,

> . . . no benefit day or play whatsoever shall be con-
> sented to or agreed by the s^d R. Wilks, etc. without
> the person who hath the same depositing into the hands
> of the treasurer of the said office of the Theatre
> Royal the sume of _forty pounds_, and such actors whose
> salary do not amount to four pounds per week (_in case_
> _such_ _have_ _benefit_ _days_) to leave (besides the said sum
> of forty pounds as aforesaid) in the hands of the s^d
> treasurer _one_ _part_ _in_ _four_ of the clear profits of such
> benefit play, and such actors who have not above fifty
> shillings per week, _a_ _full_ _third_ _part_ of the clear pro-
> fits . . . to remain in the hands of the s^d treasurer
> for the use and benefit of the s^d patent and of the
> business in general.[116]

Also, the number of benefit nights was to be limited to nine.
Summing up, we can see that all actors having a benefit had to put
up ₺40--there was nothing essentially new about this. Those earning over ₺4 per week need not share the profits above ₺40; those
earning over ₺4 a week, in addition to the ₺40 charges, would have
to give one-fourth of the remaining profits to the managers; and
actors earning 50 shillings or less a week would have to give
one-third of the clear profits to the managers. For the leading
actors who earned ₺4 a week and would ordinarily have first crack
at the benefits, the conditions were not so bad; for the lesser
actors it was a very unfortunate arrangement.

Before he attempted to share in the actors´ benefit profits,
Rich, who was not a signatory to Brett´s agreement with the
actor-managers, took the precautionary step of requiring any actor
to sign a paper stating that he voluntarily accepted a reduction
of one-third of the profits (after charges had been deducted) of
his benefit night, "any Claims from Custom, to contrary notwithstanding," as Cibber wrote. (_Apology_, p. 219) However, he changed
some of the provisions: instead of nine benefit nights, he allowed
as many as twenty between February 24 and May 1; and he insisted
that the actors deposit ₺40 with the treasurer before their benefit. When, quite understandably, several of the leading actors
refused to sign, those on the next level were offered the chance
on the same conditions, and some did agree in order to obtain the
more desirable early benefit dates. The stubborn ones reluctantly
signed, deciding not to complain to the Lord Chamberlain until the
principal benefits were over.

But in the meantime all kinds of machinations were going on,
apparently with the connivance of the Lord Chamberlain, the Earl
of Kent. It seems strange that Kent should participate so fully
in the effort to discomfort Rich; ordinarily one would expect the
Lord Chamberlain to maintain a more or less impartial stance. But

Kent's bias against Rich had apparently been exacerbated by Rich's repeatedly ignoring a series of orders that Kent had been issuing to him since March, 1707 (n.s.).[117] Of course, one reason for Rich's not responding to the orders was his belief--a belief which seems not to be anywhere contradicted in law--that the patent, derived as it was from the King, was not under the Lord Chamberlain's control. Unknown to Rich, the Lord Chamberlain approved of a certain number of the Drury Lane actors such "as might be thought fit to head a Company," secretly contracting with Owen Swiney, then directing the opera at the Haymarket. (Apology, p. 219) The chosen few--Wilks, Doggett, Mrs. Oldfield and Cibber--were to manage the new company, which would play at the Haymarket, and to be sharers with Swiney. Betterton at age 73 preferred not to be associated in the management, and both Mrs. Barry and Mrs. Bracegirdle had retired. Barton Booth, later to form with Wilks and Cibber the famous triumvirate that was to take over Drury Lane in 1714 and to govern it so successfully for sixteen years, was offered a substantial increase in salary to join but he refused. With Rich he would now have a splendid choice of outstanding roles and, in addition he would serve as a "schematist" for Rich. (Apology, p. 220) If this is so, it seems quite possible that Rich knew of this plan to desert him. Indeed, it is hard to conceive how so many people could be involved in such a plot without Rich's finding out about it. But I have not seen any document that states directly he was familiar with, or indeed ignorant of, the impending desertion. Doggett, one of the four new prospective actor-managers of the Haymarket (along with Swiney), had misgivings about a woman's sharing the direction, and so Mrs. Oldfield, one of the many victims of 18th century sexism, agreed to surrender her managerial rights in return for Ł200 a year and a clear benefit. On March 10, 1709 Swiney and the three actors signed the contract, which was supposed to endure for the fourteen years that remained before Swiney's lease of the Haymarket expired. The other details need not concern us, since our interest lies principally in Rich, but I should note a flurry of written agreements between Swiney and a number of other actors in March, April, May, June, and September, many at very generous salaries.[118]

Let us return now to the catalytic issue of deductions from actors' benefits, which in practice always seems to involve a one-third deduction from the clear profits and was commonly called the "indulto"--in Spain the indulto was a tax on all imported goods; the beneficiary was the king.[119] Rich made no effort to deduct anything from Wilks, who enjoyed the first benefit of the season on February 24, and took in Ł131.[120] But from Mrs. Oldfield's benefit, on March 3, whose receipts were over Ł134, Rich ordered the treasurer, Zachary Baggs, to deduct the expected Ł40 and one-third of the remainder. Thus, he was taking a total of ₤71 "for the use of the Patent." Thereupon, undoubtedly by prearrangement with the four conspirators (Swiney, Cibber, Wilks, Doggett), she complained to the Lord Chamberlain. When the Lord Chamberlain asked him for an explanation, Rich answered that the indulto was entirely legal, that Mrs. Oldfield had signed a document agreeing to it, and that although in her complaint she had stated that she was receiving ₤4 a week (and perhaps by implication that she was therefore exempt from the indulto) her 1703 articles, the last contract she had signed with Rich, called for only 50 shillings a week. It was Rich's generosity that increased her salary to ₤4 a week. How, therefore, could he be treating her unfairly?[121] Other actors whose benefits followed Mrs. Oldfield's also protested against the indulto to the Lord Chamberlain, and on April 30 he ordered Rich to pay the actors the full receipts of their benefits less the customary ₤40 house charges.[122] The altercation between Rich and Lord Chamberlain did not escape public notice. Richard Steele in The Tatler (No. 12) for May 7 describes Rich as the "most skilful of all politicians: he has a perfect art in being unintelligible in discourse and uncomeatable in business." Rich paid as little attention to Steele's caustic evaluation as he did to the Lord Chamberlain's command, and the conspirators did not immediately press their case against him since they were occupied in gaining the allegiance of the other actors to their cause. In the next few weeks, not hearing any further from the Lord Chamberlain, Rich grew more confident and, according to Cibber, punished those who had complained about the indulto by assigning their parts in revived plays to "loyal"-- i.e., non-complaining--actors, and by demonstrating a visible "Partiality" in promoting the loyalists. (Apology, p. 221) But the day of reckoning was at hand. Cibber, the most active of the conspirators in winning the Lord Chamberlain to their side, went to his office on June 6. There he was shown the signed order which noted that on April 30 the Lord Chamberlain had directed Rich to give the actors the full receipts for their benefits, "And whereas I am informed y^t in contempt of the Said Ord^r. y^u still refuse to pay and detain from the S^d. Comedians ye profits of ye S^d benefit plays I do therefore for the S^d. Contempt hereby Silence you from further Acting."[123] Cibber at once dashed back to Drury Lane where a play in which he had a part was in rehearsal. Rich, having noticed Cibber's absence (which would indicate Rich was attending the rehearsal), "something hastily" questioned him about his "Neglect of Business." Cibber "with an erected Look, and a Theatrical Spirit," retorted: "Sir, I have now no more Business Here, than you have; in half an Hour, you will neither have Actors to command, nor Authority, to employ them." Somewhat taken aback, Rich softened "his Reproof into a cold formal Declaration, That if he would not do his Work, he should not be paid." As if upon cue, a gentleman arrived "with the Order of Silence in his Hand." Cibber "officiously" introduced the man to Rich as a messenger

from the Lord Chamberlain. The man then delivered the order and
Cibber, exultantly "throwing his Head over his Shoulder, towards
the Patentee, in the manner of Shakespear's Harry the Eighth to
Cardinal Wolsey cry'd Read o'er that! and now--to Breakfast, with
what Appetite you may." Then all those actors who had joined with
Swiney walked out of the theatre. (Apology, pp. 221-22) So ended
the season of 1708-09 for the legitimate theatres; so ended for
several months Drury Lane's theatrical life; and, more signifi-
cantly for us, so ended forever Christopher Rich's active management of a performing theatrical company.

But of course he was not aware of this on that fateful June
6. Cibber describes Rich as a kind of bulldog, holding on with
grim tenacity to his patent: "He had no more Regard to Blows, than
a blind Cock of the Game; he might be beaten, but would never
yield, the Patent was still in his Possession, and the Broad-Seal
to it visibly as fresh as ever." (Apology, p. 223) However, at
the time Rich's optimism had some justification. No previous
silencing had lasted very long, and, as he constantly maintained,
the patentees were not obliged to submit to an order of the Lord
Chamberlain disposing of their money without their consent. The
Lord Chamberlain, Rich pointed out, was not mentioned in the
letters patent.[124] And Rich still possessed something of a company: Booth had persuaded some actors to resist Swiney's blandish-
ments, and other actors who had not been invited to the Haymarket
also remained. Further, the actors he retained did not draw very
large salaries and he could avoid paying the salaries of those who
had left him. The size of those salaries and the additional
increments the actors had received at Drury Lane in the 1708-09
season irked Rich keenly, not only because he thought no actors
deserved so much, but because the actors who had left him
presented to the public a picture of suffering, almost indigent,
performers grossly underpaid. To disabuse the town, Rich had
Zachary Baggs, Drury Lane treasurer, prepare a satirical pamphlet,
Concerning the Poor Actors, who under Pretence of hard Usage from
the Patentees, are about to desert their Services. Baggs showed
that between salary, benefits (even reduced as they were) and
extra income (which he estimated) the actors were actually very
well compensated: Wilks received almost ₤300 for 100 performances;
Betterton ₤637 for 16; Estcourt ₤364 for 52; Cibber ₤213 for 71;
Mills almost ₤91; and Mrs. Oldfield ₤252 for 39.[125] And they
would have received substantially more had it not been for Prince
George's death, which closed the theatre for 12 weeks (in reality,
only about seven). This defense of the indulto he supplemented by
reactivating old legal cases for breach-of-contract against a few
of the actors.[126] And while he was conducting this running battle
with the deserting actors, all through the summer he persisted in
his belief that he would be able to play the next season. Rich's
intransigence was noted by Alexander Pope. In a letter written on

83

August 29 he gave his opinion that the "afflicted Subjects of France" as depicted in a Tory newspaper, The Postman, do not so "grievously deplore the obstinacy of their arbitrary monarch; as these perishing People of Drury the Obdurate Heart of that Pharaoh, Rich, who like him, disdains all Proposals of Peace & Accommodation!"[127] On September 6 (we are still in 1709) the obdurate-hearted Rich, hopeful if not optimistic, attempted to open a new season, but Kent would not allow it. The Post-Boy for 13-15 September noted that "the Players were just going to act, but were, by Order from their Superiors, stopp'd from further Proceeding; so that they were, to their great Mortification, forced to dismiss their public Auditors."[128]

Not everyone was as inflexible as Rich. One who was not, and who decided to play an active role in the embroiled affairs of Drury Lane, was William Collier, an M.P. from Truro, Cornwall, a devoted Tory with influence at court, "a Lawyer of an enterprizing Head, and a jovial Heart," and possessor of a minor share in the patent. (Apology, p. 229) Just what share he owned I have not been able to ascertain; it could not have been very much, since Skipwith owned 3/5 and Rich 1/6 and there were others who also owned a small share. As a lawyer, patentee, and a power of sorts behind the throne, he could be expected to take an interest in the contretemps. He contributed £25 a week to help support the idle actors, undoubtedly a generosity not without an ulterior motive. He seems to have made friends with Sir Thomas Skipwith, who had somewhat similar ideas on how to deal with the distressing situation. In a September 13 letter to Barton Booth (now the leader of the actors who remained at Drury Lane), Collier expressed his surprise that there was an interruption to playing. From it we learn that the patentees (the performance had been advertised by the "gentleman concerned under the Patents") had thought that Sir John Stanley (secretary to Kent) had agreed to let the company act after one of its members had been arrested and that he would then "be bailed in order to try the validity of the Lord Chamberlains order against the Patents. . . ." Professors Milhous and Hume deduce that Kent had changed his mind, not wishing to try the case in court, or that the plan had been Stanley's and Kent had decided to countermand it.[129] Collier confided to Booth that there was a secret in the affair, and he gave it as his opinion that the only thing to do was to petition the Queen. From the letter we also learn that Collier was not in London, but in the country, and would be unable to come to town before October. He told Booth that whatever Rich, a Mr. Goodall, a Mr. Metcalfe "and the rest of the gentlemen concerned think fit to doe I will consent too for Sir Thomas Skipwith and myselfe," which suggests that Goodall and Metcalfe, and some others who constituted "the rest," all had some shares in the patent.[130] Matters, he continued, "are carried now soe high that I think it impracticable to sue for favours by another method than the Rule of Westminster Hall only first to peticon the Queen that her Majestie will be pleased to try our right under the ancestors Pattent." He assured Booth that he would do all he could to "keep" him and the others that stand by the patent, in spite of any private interest. He concluded with effusive praise of the Queen and restated his confidence that she would do the right thing. At the time of this letter, it is clear that Collier supported Rich's position. As Collier's letter suggested, a number of the patentees and building shareholders--nineteen in all are listed on the petition including Rich, Skipwith and Collier himself--did appeal to the Queen. They traced the histories of the Killigrew and Davenant patents, cited their rights under them, and pointed to their substantial financial involvement in the company "in Scenes, Machines, Apparell, and otherwise, amounting to above twenty thousand Pounds."[131] They noted that until the actors' revolt in 1695 their clear profits averaged ₤1000 a year, but since that time they had been "yearly considerable loosers," but not wishing to trouble the Queen, had abstained from filing a complaint. They were not aggressive; all they asked was a hearing "as to the Legality of, Releife against the said Orders; so that your Pet^{rs}. may . . . Enjoy, and Exercise the Powers, Priviledges, and Authorities Granted by the Letters Patents."

When Collier returned to London he was advised that the patents were of no effect unless they were supported by the Crown. Upon learning this, he and Sir Thomas Skipwith determined not to join the other patentees in opposing the Queen's wishes. Thus, there was a rift between the two groups of patentees: Collier and Skipwith, the practical ones, willing to bend; Rich and the others adamantly refusing to compromise. Collier was then informed that the Queen would be pleased to give leave to act to those who had claims under the patents and agreed to submit to her.[132] Thereupon Collier and Skipwith declared their submission before the Lord Chamberlain. Collier surrendered his "Claim and Interest" in the patents and on November 19 the Queen was "graciously pleased" to grant a license to act comedy and tragedy at Drury Lane. It was specifically stated in the license that Collier was not to allow Rich or any other person claiming to be concerned under the Letters Patent to have any concern at all in the management of the company. In a letter written to Collier on the same day, the Lord Chamberlain told him the good news and cautioned him not to act before Wednesday, November 23. Skipwith, though he was allied with Collier--considering the shares each held, we might say that Collier was allied with Skipwith--was not mentioned in the license. What changes had been wrought at Drury Lane in such a short period of time! Rich was specifically forbidden to participate in the management, Skipwith was not mentioned in the new license, and a minor patentee who had entered the picture just a

85

few months ago was now in control.

Let me leave Collier, happily possessed of a license, so that I can backtrack a few months and relate the activities of Owen Swiney, one-time friend and assistant of Rich, and now the manager of the Haymarket, who doubted that Rich was going to be able to revivify his patent. (Of course this was before Collier became involved.) Swiney hoped that the two companies--one for opera, one for plays--would be united under his direction and would occupy two different theatres, the Haymarket which he together with Cibber, Wilks, and Doggett already had under lease, and the now silenced Drury Lane. In an effort to obtain that playhouse he inserted the following notice in the *Daily Courant* of August 11:

> All persons who have any concern or property in the shares of rent of Drury Lane Playhouse are desired to meet Mr. Swiney at Nando's Coffee-House within Temple Bar (upon Tuesday next, the 16th instant, at 3 oclock in the afternoon), who will make 'em very advantageous proposals relating to the said house.

But the advertisement apparently proved fruitless, and Swiney *et al*, instead of dickering to take over Drury Lane, concentrated upon improving the acoustics of the Haymarket by lowering the ceiling and narrowing its width (*Apology*, p. 226), and bolstering their company by signing a few more actors.[133] In addition Swiney tried to persuade the Lord Chamberlain and the Vice Chamberlain to attach the Drury Lane actors to the Haymarket, and he was surprised and deeply disturbed when he learned of Collier's license. He wrote to the Lord Chamberlain about the desperate plight he found himself in and asserted his need to retain "all her Majesty's sworn Comedians" if the Haymarket were to be self-supporting. He hinted that the Lord Chamberlain should terminate the license.[134] Shortly afterward he was less demanding: he would be content if the license were continued if he could have a written list of performers in opera and comedy assigned to the Haymarket and the right to reduce the salaries he had originally agreed to pay them since those salaries were established when no rival company was envisioned.[135] Of course the patentees were also very much displeased with the new arrangement.

Now back to Collier. Armed with a license to perform, he approached Drury Lane's building shareholders, and by increasing the daily rent from the Ŀ3 that Rich had paid to Ŀ4 (the rent was to be paid only on nights when there were performances), he quickly persuaded them to approve him as a tenant. As for the actual possession of the house itself, that the shareholders "left to his own Cost, and Discretion." It should be noted that Collier did not gain the approval of *all* the shareholders. It is certain that Rich himself owned two of the 36 building shares, and his close friend Rupert Clarke one. They would hardly have voted to accept Collier's proposal. But all or most of the large share- holders, such as Charles Killigrew with 9, George Morley with 4 1/2, and Margaret Lacy with 4, must have agreed to it.[136] Later we know that Collier actually paid rent to the shareholders, excluding Rich, who refused to accept his share.

Rich unquestionably knew that his hold on Drury Lane was a precarious one and that an attempt to drive him from it might occur at any moment. Since it was no secret that Collier had been authorized to begin acting on November 23, Rich could anticipate an effort by Collier and his forces to attempt to seize the thea- tre before then. He may have guessed, or may have received intel- ligence from an informer, that Collier and company planned to besiege on November 22. The night before--adopting Richard Steele's imaginative account in The Tatler, No. 99 (November 26, 1709)--

> the refuse of Divito's followers [Divito, as I have already stated, is the name Steele uses for Rich in the pages of The Tatler] marched off . . . disguised in magnificence; door-keepers came out clad like cardi- nals, and scene-drawers like heathen gods. Divito him- self was wrapped in one of his black clouds, and left to the enemy nothing but an empty stage, full of trap- doors, known only to himself and his adherents.

Cibber reports that Rich "carried off every thing, that was worth moving, except a great Number of old Scenes . . . that could not easily follow him." (Apology, p. 229) Rich left behind 28 front scenes, 80 wing scenes, "several scene frames as well as other goods and things commonly made use of in the acting of plays there."[137] Not included in the goods that remained were the "cloaths," so costly to replace, so necessary in a performance.

It is a nice legal question whether Rich was entitled to abduct so many of the properties and the costumes from Drury Lane. Who really owned them? It would seem that the patentees owned them, and probably, therefore, Rich was entitled to a 1/6 part of them. Collier, as the holder of an insignificant part of the patent, might have been entitled to a miniscule part of the pro- perties and costumes. Skipwith, the majority holder of the patent, was entitled to most of them. And if he sided with Col- lier, which it seems clear he did, then we must wonder at the legality of Rich's seizure, although I have found no indication that any suit was instituted to recover them.

Whatever the legalities, Collier was not aware of them until the following evening (November 22), when, "it being a day of publick rejoyceing," he had a bonfire built in front of the theatre. To fuel it he provided "faggots, tubs, and other combustible matter," and to fuel the actors in the company he provided money so they might get properly soused drinking healths to the Queen, to the Lord Chamberlain, and to the commemoration of the victory scored on November 22. With fire inside them and out, the players cheered as Collier showed them the letter of Sir John Stanley (the Lord Chamberlain's secretary) and announced they might begin to act as soon as they pleased. Then Collier and some of the actors, as well as "a Corporal and divers Soldiers armed with swords and Musquett, in a riotous and violent manner broke open the Doors" of Drury Lane, turned out those employees of Rich that they found there, and Collier proclaimed that he took possession of the playhouse for himself and that he had Her Majesty's order for what he did.[138] With amazing dispatch, the company somehow succeeded in putting on a play (Dryden's famous heroic tragedy Aureng-Zebe) the next night, although because they lacked the customary costumes, they had to perform in their own clothes.

Let us now look at the 1709-10 season as Rich might have looked at it from the perspective of an observer, for the first time since 1693, rather than an active participant. "For years everybody has been accusing me of desecrating the stage and mistreating the actors. Now that my theatre's been taken away from me, and I've no role to play, let's see how things improve without me," he might have grumbled. Was Higgins, the contortionist who "turns himself into such a variety of Amazing Shapes and Figures, that the particulars would be incredible to all Persons who have not seen him" such an improvement?[139] He gave nine much applauded performances on the Haymarket stage during November. Was the Turkish entertainment "as it was perform'd in the Seraglio at Constantinople" given by Drury Lane on February 2 such an improvement? (Avery, p. 211) And what about the child of four who recited the prologue at Drury Lane on March 11? (Avery, p. 215) Can these "pollutions" be charged to Rich? And were there any outstanding dramatic offerings? Not unless you consider Charles Shadwell's The Fair Quaker of Deal a lasting work of art. It was the only really successful play of 1709-10 and helped Collier's company to survive. And--blame the trial of Dr. Sacheverell if you like--the Haymarket lost ₤206 on the season, despite its outstanding company and the late start of Drury Lane.[140] And what about the relations between the managers and the performers? All sweetness and light? Not at all. At the Haymarket, the actors were discontent becuase dramatic performances were limited to four nights a week. Some of the singers, especially Nicolini, one of the Italian castrati, were enraged at Swiney because he forced them to sing in some of the entr'acte entertainment when, as

88

Nicolini alleged, their contracts called for their singing only in operas. But the situation at the Haymarket was ideal compared to the altercations at Drury Lane. Collier had little interest in, and even less knowledge of, operating a theatre, and had appointed seven of the better known actors (among them Barton Booth, John Bickerstaff, Theophilus Keene, George Powell, and Francis Leigh) to manage the company for him. But when they did not meet his expectations, Collier replaced them with a budding young playwright, Aaron Hill. It was not a wise choice. Quite naturally, the ex-managers strongly resented their removal, and two in particular, Bickerstaff and Keene, were notably vocal in expressing their displeasure. The lesser actors in general, as Aaron Hill relates in a revealing letter he wrote to Collier about June 5, 1710,[141] were happy with the change and worked more diligently. To be director of rehearsals Hill first appointed George Pack, but after a day or two he "threw up ye Concern." Then Hill offered the job to Booth, "who with an Insolence, peculiar to his Nature, refus'd it, unless They might, all seven, be restor'd to their management." Finally, Hill called on his brother, Gilbert, to conduct the rehearsals. The prominent actors in the company had little respect for either brother. When Aaron left London briefly, the actors "all in an uproar, at being forfeited . . . flung up Their Parts, refus'd to act, threaten'd to take ye Cloaths out of ye House, &c. . . ." Upon Aaron's return an unidentified person who attempted to chide Bickerstaff was beaten "blind" and Bickerstaff also threatened to push brother Gilbert "off the stage by ye shoulders . . . [and] with Keene endeavour'd to disorder, & distract ye whole Company." These two violent actors, together with Booth and Leigh, publicly defied Hill, insulting him, inserting their names in the bills, challenging anyone to prevent them from entering the theatre, and determining who should act on what night. Had anything similar happened under Rich's governance? But there's more to come. Aaron received several anonymous letters telling him of "designs upon ye House, ye Cloaths, &c. . . ." Accordingly, he ordered one Stockwell, a theatre employee, to keep the house closed that night (Friday, June 2) until he (Hill) could obtain a "Guard of Constables to keep ye Peace & protect him from being insulted in his Duty. . . ." But at four that hectic afternoon Booth, Powell, Keene and several others, having entered the theatre through the lodgings of an actress, Mrs. Bradshaw (both the lodgings and the actress were attached to the playhouse), broke open "ye great Doors within," and burst into Hill's office with drawn swords in their hands. He escaped into open passage, and drew his own sword. Crowds entered the passage. Powell shortened his sword to stab Hill in the back, and cut through the hand of a gentleman who tried to prevent the thrust. Leigh, in the meantime, while brother Gilbert was being held, "struck him a dangerous Blow on ye Head, with a stick, from behind." Had all this occurred onstage the spectators would have

89

declared it absolutely improbable. Some people who had come to see the play observed all this, Hill reports. Just about this time who "happened" to pass by but Christopher Rich himself? How was he greeted by the actors? He "was huzza´d along ye Passage, had his Hands kiss´d, & was saluted by mr Leigh--God bless you, Master, see here! we are at work for you." Hill continues, "I give you but a tenth Part of ye History of These worthy Gentlemen´s Proceedings. The Cloaths that are not gone already, are to be sent away tomorrow night, & mr Rich is to be offer´d Possession of ye House, if he thinks fit to take it."

Did Rich play any part in this insurrection? In a letter supposedly but definitely not written by John Downes, the former prompter, and printed in The Tatler, no. 193, July 1 to July 4, 1710, it was alleged that Rich had not been idle "but secretly fomented divisions, and wrought over to his side some of the inferior actors. . . ." While the actors mentioned are certainly not inferior, it seems entirely plausible that Rich was somehow involved in the rebellion. I have found no evidence that Rich instigated it--for obvious reasons written materials connected with such insidious activities would not be readily accessible-- but it is entirely consistent with his character and beliefs. He had "the cause and will and strength and means." Nevertheless, we should remember that the actors were not easily gulled, and certainly must have preferred working for Rich, whatever his deceitful and tyrannical practices, to working for Collier and his surrogates.

One of the results of the rebellion was an order some twelve days after it (on June 14, 1710) by the new Lord Chamberlain, Charles Talbot, Duke of Shrewsbury, who had succeeded the Earl of Kent in April, that Powell be dismissed and that Booth, Keene, Bickerstaff, and Leigh be suspended from further acting.

In the same tumultuous month that Collier was ejected from Drury Lane and Rich seized physical possession of the playhouse, he continued to hope that the Order of Silence imposed on him would be withdrawn and that he would be able to resume his control over Drury Lane. On July 6 he signed a new lease on the land on which the theatre stood, land owned by the Duke of Bedford.[142] Rich had leased the site earlier, on September 20, 1703, as was mentioned in our discussion of the 1702-03 season. But it became increasingly clear that the silencing would stand. Sometime in late September, one "GB", seemingly on behalf of the Drury Lane building shareholders who were losing money every night the playhouse was dark, petitioned the Lord Chamberlain for a license to act, pointing out their heavy losses and noting that Rich, who possessed the scenes and clothes, without which the company could not perform, had agreed to surrender them to GB (quite probably in

90

return for some kind of compensation) were the company granted permission to act.[143]

Even after Rich's withdrawal from active pursuit of the Drury Lane management for the 1710-11 season, matters were far from settled. It was not until November that Collier was granted permission to conduct operas at the Haymarket and Swiney, joined by Wilks, Cibber, and Doggett, was given a license to operate a now united acting company, but also at the Haymarket and for only four nights a week, and one of those nights was not Saturday, the best-attended night. Performances began on October 4 at the Haymarket, but only three plays were given in the first week of that month before there was a hiatus. Acting resumed on November 4 at the Haymarket while further discussion was carried on about utilizing Drury Lane. On November 15 Collier obtained a lease from the "Major part of the Rentors" of Drury Lane and assigned it to the actor-managers.[144] Finally, on November 20, they moved to the Theatre Royal and began a monopoly on drama that was to last until late in 1714.

NOTES
Chapter 2: Rich the Manager

[1]Hotson, p. 300.

[2]Van Lennep, p. 452, quotes from Scott's preface.

[3]Gildon, English Dramatick Poets, p. 121, as quoted by Van Lennep, p. 452.

[4]Van Lennep, p. 454.

[5]See the article by Maximillian E. Novak, "The Closing of Lincoln's Inn Fields Theatre in 1695," Restoration and 18th Century Theatre Research, 14, No. 1 (May, 1975), 51-52.

[6]See Nicoll, I, 367-68, from L.C. 7/3.

[7]Quoted from A Comparison Between the Two Stages, pp. 124-25.

[8]See PRO L.C. 7/3 and Judith Milhous, Thomas Betterton and The Management of Lincoln's Inn Fields, 1695-1708 (Carbondale, Illinois: Southern Illinois University Press, 1979), p. 84.

[9]See PRO L.C. 5/152, p. 40 and Milhous, Thomas Betterton, p. 85.

[10]Van Lennep, p. 470, quoting from a letter written on Nov. 19, 1696, by Robert Jennens to Thomas Coke.

[11]So declares the title page of the 1697 edition of the play. See Van Lennep, p. 479.

[12]Here is the puff from the Post Boy:

Great Preparations are making for a new Opera in the
Play-house in Dorset-Garden, of which there is great
Expectation, the Scenes being several new Sets and of a
moddel [sic] different from all that have been used in
any Theatre whatever, being twice as high as any of
their former Scenes. And the whole Decoration of the
Stage not only infinitely beyond all the Opera's ever
yet performed in England, but also by the acknowledgment of several Gentlemen that have travell'd abroad,
much exceeding all that been seen on any of the Foreign
Stages.''

[13]The World in the Moon; an Opera, as it is perform'd at the Theatre in Dorset Garden. 2nd ed. (London: 1697).

[14] See Apology, p. 225, and, based on Cibber's account, The Theatre Royal. . . Covent Garden, p. 45.

[15] In somewhat greater detail Van Lennep, p. 496, quotes from the 1698 edition of the play.

[16] See Animadversions on Mr. Congreve's late Answer to Mr. Collier (1698), pp. 34-35, quoted by Van Lennep, p. 486.

[17] Nicoll, I, 368 and Van Lennep, pp. 494-95.

[18] A Comparison Between the Two Stages, p. 22.

[19] See PRO C8,599/74. In my account of the litigation between the patentees and the Earl of Dorset in regard to Dorset Garden, I follow Judith Milhous, Thomas Betterton, pp. 109, 121-22.

[20] A Comparison Between the Two Stages, pp. 25-26.

[21] Roscius Anglicanus, p. 45.

[22] This is the opinion of Lady Marow in a letter dated March 12, 1699 (o.s.) quoted by Van Lennep, p. 526.

[23] Roscius Anglicanus, p. 45.

[24] Letters of John Dryden, p. 131, as quoted by Van Lennep, p. 520.

[25] See his letter to George Moult quoted at some length by Van Lennep, pp. 515-16.

[26] The Patentee was published in London in 1700.

[27] Quoted by Van Lennep, p. 529.

[28] Nicoll, I, 382, prints the contract.

[29] See John Vanbrugh's letter of Dec. 25, 1699 to the Earl of Manchester, quoted by Van Lennep, p. 521.

[30] See the preface to the play, which was printed in 1700. It is quoted at some length by Van Lennep, pp. 531-32.

[31] A Comparison Between the Two Stages, p. 12.

[32] A Comparison Between the Two Stages, p. 12.

[33]See Post Boy, for March 22-25, quoted by Emmett L. Avery, ed., The London Stage 1660-1800, Part 2: 1700-1729, (Carbondale, Illinois: Southern Illinois University Press, 1960), p. 9.

[34]Apology, p. 126. This judgment, of course, was published more than 35 years after the event.

[35]See Nicoll, I, p. 340, based on L.C. 5/153, p. 22.

[36]The lines are reprinted in Milhous, Thomas Betterton, p. 130.

[37]The pamphlet, The State of the Case . . . Restated (1720), is quoted by Arthur Colby Sprague, Beaumont and Fletcher on the Restoration Stage (1926; rpt. New York: Blom, 1965), pp. 85-86. See also Milhous, Thomas Betterton, pp. 131, 267.

[38]See PRO C10/364/8, summarized by Hotson, p. 307.

[39]Apology, p. 184. But the London debut of elephants was only a few years away. One nine- to ten-foot-high elephant from Guinea appeared at Pinkeman's Booth in Brookfield Market-Place at the East Corner of Hyde Park in May, 1704. It remained for 16 days. See Avery, p. 66.

[40]Nicoll, II, 292, from L.C. 7/3.

[41]For two lists of the building sharers, see The Theatre Royal . . . Covent Garden, pp. 12-13. In 1695 the four leading shareholders were Killigrew (9), Penelope Morley (4 1/2), William Clayton (4), and Margaret Lacy (4). Twelve other names are cited. In 1710-11, Killigrew and Lacy had retained their shares, George Morley had the 4 1/2 Penelope had owned, Rich himself had two, and his long-time associate, Rupert Clarke, had one. Eleven other names are mentioned, including two trustees.

[42]For information on Killigrew's early suits, see PRO C6/438/55 (April 1700) and C10/297/57 (n.d., about 1700). See also the discussion in Milhous, Thomas Betterton, p. 122. I follow Milhous in much of my account of events connected with Killigrew's suits against Rich.

[43]See Hotson, p. 273, for some details of this lease.

[44]See PRO C10/261/51, Killigrew et al vs. Skipwith and Rich, bill of complaint, and Milhous, Thomas Betterton,

p. 122.

[45]See PRO C10/261/51, Answer, 4 February "1702/3" and Milhous, _Thomas Betterton_, pp. 122-24 and note 14, p. 266.

[46]See "The Case of the Building Proprietors," n.d. The document is at the Bedford Office, 29A Montague Street, London, W.C. 1.

[47]See Hotson, p. 306 and _The Theatre Royal_ . . . _Covent Garden_, p. 31.

[48]_The Players turn'd Academicks: or, A Description_ (_In Merry Metre) Of their Translation From the Theatre in Little Lincoln's-Inn-Fields, to the Tennis-Court in Oxford_ (London: 1703), p. 11.

[49]See Avery's entries, for Dec. 31, Feb. 7, July 26, and Aug. 11. His son John was to adopt the same practice 20 years later.

[50]I base my account largely on Milhous, _Thomas Betterton_, pp. 152-59, and Hotson, pp. 300-02, 324-25. Smith's original bill is PRO C8/599/74. He was joined in his suit by William Shiers, Thomas Savery and Robert Gower. Subsequent bills were C8/599/77; C8/604/6; C8/604/5; C8/629/34; C8/620/35. These date from 1704 to 1708 and the defendants are all associated with Drury Lane or Lincoln's Inn Fields. One, C5/337/72, concerns only Lincoln's Inn Fields actors.

[51]Hotson, p. 302.

[52]Verbruggen's petition can be found in PRO L.C. 7/3. Milhous, _Thomas Betterton_, reprints it (pp. 252-54) and discusses it (pp. 160-61).

[53]_Thomas Betterton_, p. 157.

[54]Nicoll, II, p. 275.

[55]See Milhous, _Thomas Betterton_, p. 194, from which I take a number of details. She mentions that a letter dated November 27, 1704, instructing Rich not to meddle, is among the papers in L.C. 7/3.

[56]See Clayton's preface to _Arsinoe, Queen of Cyprus_ (London: Tonson, 1705). Milhous, _Thomas Betterton_, pp. 195-96, prints a brief excerpt.

[57] Avery, p. 85.

[58] Milhous, _Thomas Betterton_, p. 195.

[59] See Roger Fiske, _English Theatre Music in the Eighteenth Century_ (1973; London: Oxford University Press), p. 3.

[60] See Milhous, _Thomas Betterton_, p. 200. She quotes from Daniel Defoe in his _Review of the Affairs of France_ for May 3, 1705: ". . . the Founders of this Structure . . . Complain of Deficient Funds for the Compleating the Building."

[61] _Roscius Anglicanus_, p. 198.

[62] _Roscius Anglicanus_, p. 48.

[63] _Love for Love_ was played on June 25, 27; _Rule a Wife and Have a Wife_ on June 8. See Avery, pp. 95-97.

[64] Quoted by Richard H. Barker, _Mr. Cibber of Drury Lane_ (1939; rpt. New York: AMS Press, 1966), p. 63.

[65] Barker, p. 63.

[66] Quoted by Avery, p. 88.

[67] See L.C. 7/3 as quoted by Nicoll, II, 289 and the preface from the printed play, excerpted by Avery, p. 90. The Queen's play was _The Consultation_, presented first on April 24.

[68] Milhous, _Thomas Betterton_, p. 197, from PRO L.C. 7/3.

[69] See "A Move [Motive] for the Censorship of Owen Swiney's 'The Quacks,'" _Notes & Queries_, 203 (1958), 393-96.

[70] _Roscius Anglicanus_, p. 48.

[71] See Congreve's letter (no. XVI) to Joseph Keally, from London, in _Literary Relics_, ed. George-Monck Berkeley (London: 1789), pp. 343-44.

[72] Downes, in _Roscius Anglicanus_, p. 49, says _The Temple of Love_ lasted six nights.

[73] Downes, p. 50, states _Wonders in the Sun_ gave six performances.

[74]See L.C. 7/3, rather fully presented by Nicoll, II, 274-75.

[75]See L.C. 7/3, reproduced in part by Nicoll, II, 290-91.

[76]This is dated Jan. 28, 1705, which is probably old style.

[77]See the summary by Nicoll, II, 289-90, based on PRO L.C. 7/3.

[78]The original letter is in the Osborn Collection, Yale University, and is reprinted by Judith Milhous and Robert D. Hume, Vice Chamberlain Coke's Theatrical Papers, 1706-1715 (Carbondale, Illinois: Southern Illinois University Press, 1982), pp. 11-13.

[79]See William Congreve: Letters & Documents, ed. John C. Hodges (New York: Harcourt, Brace, and World, 1964), No. 26. Milhous, Thomas Betterton, p. 208, quotes from this.

[80]The text is in L.C. 7/3. Milhous and Hume, Coke's Theatrical Papers, pp. 9-11, reprint and comment on this letter.

[81]Barker, p. 66.

[82]Vanbrugh is writing to the Earl of Manchester on May 11, 1708. The letter is reprinted as an interdocument by Milhous and Hume, Coke's Theatrical Papers, pp. 106-07.

[83]The date is December 9, 1706. The letter is reprinted and discussed by Milhous and Hume, Coke's Theatrical Papers, pp. 106-07.

[84]Muses Mercury or Monthly Miscellany, March, 1707, as quoted by Barker, p. 67.

[85]Fiske, English Theatre Music, p. 48.

[86]This letter is reprinted by Milhous and Hume, Coke's Theatrical Papers, pp. 16-17.

[87]See his letter and a discussion of it by Milhous and Hume, Coke's Theatrical Papers, pp. 18-19.

[88]See Barker, p. 67. He dates this as December, 1707 but the proper date must be 1706.

[89]L.C. 7/3, as quoted by Barker, p. 67.

[90]May and March.

[91]Thomas Betterton, pp. 214-15.

[92]This paragraph is adapted from Barker, p. 66, who cites as his sources C9/464/116 and 464/32; C10/528/33 and 537/22; Chancery Decrees and Orders, 1708B, p. 175.

[93]A Comparison Between the Two Stages, p. 11.

[94]Three Original Letters to a Friend in the Country, on the Cause and Manner of the Late Riot at The Theatre-Royal in Drury Lane (London: 1763), Letter III.

[95]See PRO C7 642/44. The bill (which was filed on July 3, 1707) and the answers are given, almost in their entirety, by Hotson, pp. 380-85.

[96]Apology, Chapter XI, is the source of much of the information and all of the quotations used in the paragraphs describing the activities leading up to the uniting of the two companies. Although Cibber reports that Nicolini Grimaldi's arrival in London helped persuade Swiney to accept the directorship of the opera, Nicolini seems not to have performed until the following season, 1708-1709.

[97]A poem, "On a handsom Singer, covetous and proud" (subsequently titled upon publication "On Mrs T____s"), describes her thus: "So bright is thy beauty, so charming thy song, / As had drawn both the beast and their Orpheus along; / But such is thy av'rice, and such is thy pride, / That the beasts must have starv'd, and the Poet have dy'd." It is sometimes attributed to Pope. See Milhous and Hume, Coke's Theatrical Papers, p. 110.

[98]See Milhous and Hume, Coke's Theatrical Papers, pp. 39-40.

[99]Reprinted and discussed by Milhous and Hume, Coke's Theatrical Papers, pp. 45-49.

[100]See Estcourt's letter to the Lord Chamberlain, dated by Milhous and Hume, Coke's Theatrical Papers, pp. 44-45, as probably December 29, 1707.

[101]See BL Add Ms 20726, f. 36. The order of union is most easily accessible in Milhous, Thomas Betterton,

pp. 217-18 and Milhous and Hume, Coke's Theatrical Papers, pp. 49-50.

[102]Judith Milhous and Robert D. Hume, "The Silencing of Drury Lane in 1709," Theatre Journal, 32, no. 4 (December, 1980), 427-47. The quotation is from p. 430.

[103]Vanbrugh's letter, probably written January 20, 1708, is reprinted and discussed by Milhous and Hume, Coke's Theatrical Papers, pp. 73-75.

[104]See HM 6833 in the Huntington Library, San Marino, California.

[105]Quoted by Avery, p. 165.

[106]See the appendix, Chancery Bills and Answers, in Hotson, pp. 322-25. In this same period, following the listing of cases in Hotson, Rich was also co-defendant in three suits claiming profits in the theatre had not been paid.

[107]See The Theatre Royal . . . Covent Garden, footnote, p. 12.

[108]See PRO C10/385/16. Hotson, p. 310, gives a good account of the case.

[109]Berkeley, Letter II, to Joseph Keally.

[110]The full texts of Skipwith's original complaint, and the two responses by Brett, are most readily available in Hotson, pp. 386-97.

[111]Apology, p. 214. Note that Cibber misdates his account of the litigation between Brett and Skipwith. He places Brett's resignation of the patent before Rich's silencing. Actually, it came after.

[112]I take the date of Sir Thomas' death from Fulwar Skipwith, pp. 29-30.

[113]See St. Clement Danes rate book B 4 in the Westminster Public Library, Buckingham Palace Road, London.

[114]In this season (1706-07) Penkethman is listed by Avery, p. 130, as a member of Rich's company.

[115]Nicoll, I, 369, 393.

[116] See Percy Fitzgerald, _A New History of the English Stage_ (London: 1882), II, 445. It is also printed by Milhous and Hume, "The Silencing of Drury Lane in 1709," p. 432.

[117] _The Theatre Royal . . . Covent Garden_, p. 12. The sources are L.C. 5/154, ff. 224, 298-300, 417.

[118] See Nicholl, II, pp. 286-87, for details of ten of the contracts, all taken from L.C. 7/3.

[119] _Webster's New International Dictionary of the English Language_, 2nd ed., Unabridged, defines an indulto as a duty levied by the king of Spain or Portugal on all importations.

[120] See Zachary Baggs, _Advertisement Concerning the Poor Actors, who under Pretence of hard Usage from the Patentees, are about to desert their Service_ (London: n.p., 1709), p. 2.

[121] See Barker, p. 77, based upon L.C. 7/3 and Milhous and Hume, "The Silencing of Drury Lane," pp. 433-35.

[122] See L.C. 5/154, p. 417.

[123] This is L.C. 5/154, p. 437. It is reprinted in part by Nicoll, II, 282.

[124] See BL Add Ms 20726.

[125] The pamphlet appeared on July 8. I have rounded out Baggs' figures to the nearest pound.

[126] For the defense of the indulto, see _A New History of the English Stage_ (London: 1882), I, 267-69. Barker, p. 77, refers to these pages. For reactivating the breach of contract cases, see C10/528/33 and 537/22 and Add. Ms. 38,607. Barker, p. 78, refers to these documents.

[127] _The Correspondence of Alexander Pope_, ed. George Sherburn (Oxford: Oxford University Press, 1956) I, 171. Pope is corresponding with Henry Cromwell.

[128] Quoted by Avery, pp. 198-99.

[129] Collier's letter is in BL Add Ms 20,726, ff 33-34. It is reprinted as an interdocument by Milhous and Hume, _Coke's Theatrical Papers_, pp. 125-26. Their deduction is on

p. 439 of their article, "The Silencing of Drury Lane in 1709." The protest eventually led to an order in Council, on February 18, 1710, calling for an investigation. A report on October 8, 1711 supported Rich and the other petitioners, but by then it was too late to affect what had already occurred. See Coke's Theatrical Papers, p. 124.

[130]See Folger T.a. 67 in the Folger Shakespeare Library, Washington, D.C.

[131]The petition is in BL Add Ms 20,726, ff 22-23. It is discussed, and some of it is reprinted, by Milhous and Hume, "The Silencing of Drury Lane in 1709," pp. 439-40.

[132]See BL Add Ms 20726.

[133]Nicoll, II, pp. 286-87, lists some details of a number of contracts Swiney and several performers signed.

[134]Milhous and Hume, Coke's Theatrical Papers, pp. 128-29, print and briefly discuss Swiney's letter, written sometime in November, 1709 and directed to the Vice Chamberlain.

[135]See Swiney's letter, written sometime in November, 1709, and a brief commentary by Milhous and Hume, Coke's Theatrical Papers, pp. 130-31.

[136]See BM ADD Ms 20,726, no. 5, and PRO C11/1175/59. A list of the shareholders in 1710 can be found in a footnote on p. 13, The Theatre Royal . . . Covent Garden.

[137]For a description of these variegated scenes, see C11/225/50, copied in some detail by Barker, p. 83.

[138]Details of this invasion are taken largely from BL Add Ms 20,726; a few details are also taken from The Tatler, No. 99.

[139]The Daily Courant, Dec. 7, 1709. It is quoted by both Avery, p. 206, and Barker, p. 80. Addison wrote a disapproving account of Higgins in The Tatler, No. 108, Thursday, Dec. 15 to Sat. Dec. 17.

[140]Apology, p. 230, and C7/668/31, cited by Barker, p. 81.

[141]This letter is reprinted with a commentary by Milhous and Hume, Coke's Theatrical Papers, pp. 142-46.

[142]See the records of the Trustees of the Bedford Settled Estates in the Greater London Record Office, County Hall, S.E.1 under Drury Lane, July 6, 1710 lease to C. Rich.

[143]For the petition and a commentary, see Milhous and Hume, Coke's Theatrical Papers, p. 150.

[144]See PRO C/10/261/51.

CHAPTER THREE
Frustration, Construction and Death:
Christopher Rich's Last Years (1709-1714)

As the 1710-11 season progressed with Rich as a spectator again, he realized that to resume his management he needed three things: the restoration of his patent rights, a theatre, and a company of actors, and he attempted to obtain all three more or less simultaneously. The first, the reactivation of the patent, he was not to achieve until 1714. As effort after effort failed, Rich was forced to realize that until there was a change of monarch, or at least of administration, his chances were slim indeed. But in the summer of 1710 his hopes were high enough for him to actively seek a playhouse. Lincoln's Inn Fields was clearly the logical choice. Rich had already demonstrated his interest in it a year or two ago, as the St. Clement Danes rate books indicate, even though a Daily Courant advertisement in September of 1708 stated it could not be used as a playhouse (see above, p. 62). But whoever had made that decision changed his mind in the next 11 months, because on August 12, 1709, an advertisement in the Daily Courant proclaimed that any persons "who had a mind to be concerned in or to rent the playhouse in Little Lincoln's Inn Fields" should meet with a Mr. Porcino and Mr. Sniff at Nando's Coffeehouse in Temple Bar four days later at four p.m. Apparently the restriction against using the building as a theatre had been lifted. Rich, whose name had been listed in the rate books for 1708-09, did not renew his interest, it would seem, for 1709-10 but his name does appear for 1710-11. The letter in The Tatler already referred to, putatively by Downes, tells us that Rich was already renovating the playhouse by July 1, the date of the letter. He writes about "the whole frame of the house being designed to be altered" and in a post script adds that he had been "credibly informed that they design a new house in Lincoln's Inn Fields, near the Popish chapel, to be ready by Michaelmas next; which indeed is but repairing an old one that has already failed." The term "new house" is misleading, as the letter writer suggests, since Michaelmas was September 29, and three months is hardly enough time to construct a new theatre. Rich was simply making a few improvements, altering it, and did not plan to construct a new theatre at that moment. Rich's third desideratum, a troupe, he was collecting too. That same Tatler letter informs us that he had called in "the most eminent of strollers from all parts of the Kingdom," and that its author had actually seen them "all ranged together behind the scenes." When permission to play was not forthcoming, Rich must have disbanded his actors, abandoned his idea of renovating Lincoln's Inn Fields, and definitely determined to tear it down and build a new one.

The exact date when Rich gave the order to tear down the Old Lincoln's Inn Fields playhouse I cannot state. The demolition could not have begun until the fall of 1710, but perhaps Rich delayed--there was then no need for great expedition. Nor can I state the exact date upon which actual construction of the new theatre commenced. But we do know that Rich enjoyed this kind of work, so much so that Cibber asserts Rich was little concerned by the order of silence since "it gave him so much uninterrupted Leisure to supervise a Work, which he naturally took Delight in." (Apology, p. 233) It is difficult to accept this judgment. That rebuilding a theatre pleased him I do not doubt, for such an occupation was wonderful therapy for a suddenly leisured active businessman, but I think he was genuinely concerned by the suspension of the patent and did not indulge his architectural appetite without casting an envious eye upon his rivals. Not envious of everything that occurred at the two theatres between the fall of 1710 and the fall of 1714, of course, because in many aspects the period was far from admirable. Swiney and Collier played musical chairs shifting from Drury Lane to the Haymarket and from the Haymarket to Drury, a discontinuity that did not enhance management. They quarrelled with actor-managers Cibber, Wilks and Doggett about whether they -- Swiney and Collier -- should be paid for being more or less silent partners, and if so, then how much. On several occasions Swiney complained about unauthorized withdrawls from the Drury Lane receipts by the three actor-managers; once the amount was ₤350, a second time ₤1100, which occasioned a letter by Swiney to the Lord Chamberlain.[1] Often Collier failed to pay his bills.[2] Vanbrugh tried time and again to obtain rent for the Drury Lane scenery and costumes, stock which had been taken from the Haymarket.[3] A substantial number of Drury Lane patrons--73 of them--complained that the actor-managers would not allow Laetitia Cross to perform.[4] Doggett complained incessantly, first about Barton Booth's being admitted to partnership in the Drury Lane management, later against Richard Steele's admission into partnership.[5] These and other expressions of discontent found their way into Vice Chamberlain Coke's papers; many, we assume, reached the ear of the Lord Chamberlain himself. There was litigation in the Court of Chancery. Agreements made were cancelled, new licenses were issued, recriminations were exchanged, one manager railed against another, and Swiney finally bowed out of all management about January 15, 1713.[6] He had spent large sums of money to provide new habits, decorations and scenes for a new opera, Handel's Theseus. To pay for them he tried to sell a number of subscriptions for six performances at the Haymarket but could not. So he fled to Europe, taking the receipts with him, leaving behind unpaid singers and unpaid-for scenes and clothes.[7] No, indeed, tension and turmoil on the London stage didn't stop when Rich left it.

As we have seen, backstage dissension reached one of its highs in this period between the Riches (i.e., 1709-1714), but its import would be greatly mitigated if the quality of the entertainment on the other side of the stage also approached a high. But of all the new plays presented at Drury Lane, only three deserve special mention: Nicholas Rowe's moving tragedy Jane Shore (1714), Ambrose Philips' The Distrest Mother (1712), and the somewhat wooden but very successful tragedy by Addison, Cato (1713). One might well question the literary merit of the second and the dramatic merit of the third. Nor was the opera particularly distinguished, although Handel had begun contributing to the London musical scene.

If Rich did not find the level of the new entertainments on the Drury Lane stage admirable, surely he found enviable the dramatic monopoly the Theatre Royal enjoyed, a monopoly interrupted only by Wednesday and Saturday performances of opera at the Haymarket and relatively inconsequential musical performances at small rooms, and the huge profits reaped by the new managers. Contributing to the profits was the aforementioned Cato. Addison's tragedy premiered on April 14, 1713, ran for 20 nights punctuated only by two benefit evenings; it was curtailed by the imminent parturition of Mrs. Oldfield, who played the important role of Marcia.[8] In each season the three active managers, despite paying Collier Ŀ700 for his share in the license and a Ŀ100 assessment by the Lord Chamberlain to help the opera, never earned less than Ŀ1000 each. (Apology, p. 237) In the 1712-13 season Cibber, Wilks, and Doggett each cleared Ŀ1350, and they divided another Ŀ450 for three or four crowded performances of Cato at Oxford. In 1713-14 they earned a very satisfying total of Ŀ3600, and in less than three months' playing time in the fall of 1714 they cleared Ŀ1700, the greatest profit that any English theatre had made in the autumn.[9] Profits such as these were the strongest kind of incentive for Rich to construct a new theatre in anticipation of the time when he would regain his patent rights.

In many ways our knowledge of this new theatre, the third in Lincoln's Inn Fields, is very limited. Isolated facts such as the continued appearance of Rich's name opposite the playhouse from 1710-11 through 1714-15 in the St. Clement Danes' rate books I have. In 1713-14 his given name is inscribed in front of Rich, as it was earlier recorded. And for the first time he paid taxes--Ŀ2 8s 8d for the first two quarters of 1714-15. But more important details, such as the name of the builder, who in those days was often something of an architect as well, eludes us. Some 111 years after the completion of the playhouse in 1714, a book about London theatres, Theatrum Illustrata, listed a man named Sheppard (he spelled his name Shepherd) as the architect and stated that under his direction the theatre began to be built, "though slowly,

in the year 1709-10."[10]   But when Theatrum Illustrata tells us
that "Sheppard" had "previously built the playhouse in Goodman's
Fields," a playhouse that in fact was not built until 1731, we
have to question its credibility; nor does Theatrum Illustrata
provide its sources.   Further reason to doubt that Shepherd (whose
first name is Edward) was the architect of Lincoln's Inn Fields is
that his name is not mentioned in that connection in the long,
involved and detailed account of the litigation between Shepherd
and John Rich relative to the construction in 1731 and 1732 of
Covent Garden theatre, which Shepherd did build, and which was
modeled, in many ways, on Lincoln's Inn Fields.[11]

If we know little about the theatre's architect, we know more
about its financing.   Typically at this time the construction
costs of a London theatre were paid by selling shares in the
building.   But Rich probably was unable to dispose of any shares
as work began upon the playhouse--he had no physical theatre, no
viable patent, and in the fall of 1710 did not even have a lease
on the land on which the playhouse was to stand.   In a few years
all of these things were to come, but in late 1710 and 1711 Rich
needed money to pay for the erection of the playhouse.   How did he
obtain it?   He may have had some money in a bank.   I have found no
evidence of any accounts that he had, but the absence of the positive does not prove the negative.   The banks which held his money
may have gone out of existence a few years later and their records
may have been destroyed.   It is probable he did have some money
cached away, money which he was now spending.   And he used other
means to gather funds.   He borrowed on the collateral of property
he owned.   On March 1, 1711 (n.s.) he signed an indenture of mortgage with Rupert Clarke of Lyons Inn, a man who often worked
closely with Rich in his financial deals and whom Rich trusted,
for he was named as one of his executors in his 1714 will.   All of
Rich's share in the eight acre property known as Gravel Pit fields
or pasture in St. Andrews Holborn, both land and buildings (this
was a speculation Rich had entered into with Sir Thomas Skipwith
the elder around 1687), he mortgaged to Clarke for long terms, 60
and 99 years, in return for Ь250.   If Rich were to pay back the
250 plus interest by September 2, Clarke would return the mortgage.[12]   On January 6, 1713 (n.s.) Rich borrowed Ь250 more from
Clarke, the security being the two shares (of the total of 36) of
Drury Lane theatre, which Clarke could hold for the residue of the
term of 14 years and 21 years after that.   Rich retained the right
to recover the shares if he paid Clarke the Ь250 plus interest
before July 7, 1713.[13]   This mortgage is of particular interest
because one of its witnesses was John Rich.   This is the first
time that I found John, now 21 years old, participating in his
father's business affairs.   About three months later, on April 23,
1713, Rich must have needed money badly, for he engaged, with his
friend Rupert Clarke again, in two transactions, which were

outright sales. One of the transactions suggests that Rich had made some arrangements with Clarke about paying off the ₤250 he had borrowed in 1711 with his share in Gravel Pit fields as collateral, for it is their shares in this area that Clarke and he jointly sell to John Metcalfe of St. Andrews Holborne for ₤400 for the several terms of years under which the property was leased.[14] There is no mention of buying back the property. Again his son John is a witness, as is another relative, Henry Rich, whose exact relationship I have not been able to establish. On the same day Rich and Clarke sold a messuage to Davenant Metcalfe, a spinster and almost certainly a relative of the John Metcalfe mentioned above. For the mortgage and equity of redemption of this messuage and its "appurtenances" located in Gray's Inn Lane, for the remainder of a term of 55 years, Miss Metcalfe paid ₤300 with no provision of repurchase.[15] Since John was once more one of the witnesses, we can assume that John was now in London and probably assisting Christopher in some of the work associated with building a new theatre. Perhaps they were living together, but it would be difficult to say where, based on the addresses Rich gives in these two April 13 instruments. In the Gravel Pit indenture he says he is residing in St. Martins in the Fields; in the Gray's Inn messuage sale he says he is residing in St. Pauls, Covent Garden parish. Wherever he was located, his need for money continued. He seems to have borrowed ₤200 from a man named March around this time, because he was the defendant in a Kings Bench suit for this amount. Unfortunately the membrane containing the details of this case is missing.[16] Probably before the spring of 1714 he borrowed from a Hugh Wise about ₤206, and because he failed to pay it he was named defendant in a Kings Bench suit in the same year.[17] And Rich signed a bond to repay ₤560 he was borrowing from his friend Rupert Clarke. Rich must have promised to return the money very shortly, because only a brief time passed before Clarke was suing Rich in a Kings Bench case. I particularly regret that I could find no more information about this case because the circumstances must be very unusual for one friend to sue another for a debt of only a few weeks' standing. Could it have been a piece of legal chicanery? At this time, we know, Rich was experiencing serious financial problems since he is described in the Clarke suit as being in custody in the Marshalsea prison.[18] On August 28 (1714) Rich again must have required additional funds for he borrowed ₤100 from a William Jackson, and did not return the money.[19] In all probability there were other debts and other cases in which Rich was involved which I have not unearthed. The increasing frequency of Rich's borrowings suggests his expenditures grew heavier as the theatre was constructed. But before we shed tears for Rich's economic plight, we should remember that it is, to some extent certainly, a question of a temporary shortage of cash resulting from investments in a long term capital good. He had delayed selling shares in the theatre for reasons I shall discuss later, but he could rationally expect several thousand pounds once he decided to offer them. That Rich had been hurt--seriously hurt--by the suspension of the patent rights he had been exercising no one can doubt. But that he was in imminent danger of incarceration in a debtor's prison we can also doubt.

After Rich was ejected from Drury Lane he was much less in the public eye than when he was managing the Theatre Royal and Dorset Garden. But periodically there were references to him, most notably in The Tatler and The Spectator. Not long after the silencing, which took place on June 6, 1709, Steele was presenting in The Tatler (no. 42, July 16) an imaginative list of movables belonging to Rich, who, he writes, is breaking up "housekeeping."[20] The longest reference in The Spectator occurs in No. 258, (December 26, 1711) penned by Steele, who was much more familiar with theatrical maneuvers than Addison. Rich, who was known as Divito in The Tatler, becomes Kitt Crotchet in The Spectator. Steele has a near kinsman of Kitt, Ralph Crotchet, write a letter defending rope dancers, vaulters, tumblers, ladder-walkers and posture-makers, and urges that they return to the stage for the pleasure of the many people who have active bodies without quick conceptions. Briefer references to Rich are made in numbers 5 (March 6, 1711) and 36 (April 11, 1711).

During these years of construction, Rich's personal life is largely a mystery. No longer did he associate with Cibber, our single best source of information about him. From the several references to his sons John and Christopher Mosyer in contracts we know that they were in London in 1713 and 1714, but they do not seem to be living with him, nor with each other. Since he was now well along into his sixties and his connection with actresses more tenuous than it had been, quite possibly his social life was quieter than when he and Cibber had joined in parties quarrées. What with architecture, finances and possibly legal activities, Rich may have been sufficiently occupied.

With the death of Queen Anne on August 1, 1714, the managers, present and past, were galvanized into action. The advent of George I brought the Whigs into power, and at Drury Lane Collier, an ardent Tory, was a liability, completely impotent to influence the new administration. Hence, Cibber, Wilks and Booth (who had replaced Doggett in the triumvirate of actors directing the Theatre Royal) appealed to Steele, a Whig, who had succeeded Collier as the non-acting member of the Drury Lane management, to obtain a renewal of their previous license, now about to expire. Steele begged the Duke of Marlborough to intercede for them, and a new license was issued on October 18, almost a month after the playhouse had begun its 1714-15 season (on September 21) with an appropriate prologue on His Majesty's Public Entry written by

Steele and spoken by Wilks.

Rich, of course, had a more difficult road to travel but he had every reason to hope that the restoration of the patent, denied him in Queen Anne's reign, might be granted now. Rich besought the aid of James Craggs, the younger, a shareholder in Rich's new theatre, and a man of influence who was to become Secretary of State four years later. Craggs agreed to present Rich's case before the King. So effective was Craggs that the King told him (as Craggs later told Cibber) "That he [the King] remember'd, when he had been in England before, in King Charles his time there had been Two Theatres in London; and as the Patent seem'd to be a lawful Grant, he saw no Reason, why Two Play-houses might not be continued." (Apology, p. 272) Now that it was certain Rich could perform in the new theatre, he went about preparing and signing two documents which until this moment he had felt it wise to delay. One was the indenture on August 31, 1714, by which he acquired a lease on the property on which Lincoln's Inn Fields stood. There can be little doubt that sometime before this date Rich must have come to an understanding with the three proprietors of the property: Anne Reeve of Kensington, a widow; Deodatus Champion of Plumpton, Northamptonshire, gentleman; and Thomas Reeve of the Inner Temple, London, esquire. No one, certainly not Rich, would be foolish enough to construct a playhouse on land which he could not be sure of being able to lease. It seems likely that the two Reeves and Champion, who in all probability had inherited the property, agreed to forfeit any rent until the prohibition on the patent had been relaxed.[21] Possibly there had also been some agreement on not collecting rent until the theatre had reached a certain stage of completion. But the terms of the August 31 contract Rich and his friend and seemingly close associate, Rupert Clarke of Lyons Inn, gentleman, were to pay Ł100 annually beginning on the feast day of the nativity of John the Baptist, June 24, for 39 1/2 years. In this indenture, as in the one following, Clarke probably did not participate, but simply allowed his name to be used. In another agreement it was stated that Clarke's name was only made use of in trust for Christopher Rich.[22] The August 31 indenture, which is recapitulated in some detail in a British Library document, Add. Ch. 9303, also makes it clear that some buildings on the north side of the theatre, probably used for scene storage, continued to stand more or less in their original state, and that the theatre was going to be called the New Theatre or the British Theatre.

Three days later, on September 3, Rich and Clarke made a second indenture in which they declared that the earlier contract with the Reeves and Champion had been made in trust for a number of shareholders in the theatre. And it is thus that we learn that Rich had been selling builders' shares in Lincoln's Inn Fields--or should we call it the New Theatre or the British Theatre, names by which it was never known? Probably the sale of these shares did not begin much before late summer of 1714. I can suggest two reasons for this late start: 1) it is difficult to sell shares in a theatre whose manager's patent had been rendered nugatory; 2) because--and this is a surprise--he didn't need money to defray the costs of building the theatre. According to his son John, who in 1736 was making a brief appeal to restrain the number of theatres, his father sold shares for "getting together a Company of Actors, or for the purchasing of Cloaths, Scenes, Machines, and other Things necessary for Acting."[23] John declares that his father had rebuilt the theatre in Lincoln's Inn Fields "at a very great Expence," but he sold shares only when "most of the other Persons who were interested in the Patent" refused "to contribute any Money" for the purposes I have just listed.

Rich divided the theatre into 36 parts or shares and placed them on sale for Ł120 plus the promise to pay a share of the Ł100 annual rent, in return for which he agreed to pay two shillings for every night that a play was performed in Lincoln's Inn Fields or elsewhere, "under the Authority of the said Letters Patent." At the time the second indenture was signed (September 3), Rich had disposed of 16 of the 36 shares. Among the most distinguished of the purchasers were Lionel, Earl of Dorset, and James Craggs the younger, who had helped Rich regain the use of his patent, as we have seen. John Rich, identified as a gentleman of Gray's Inn, and Christopher Mosyer Rich of London, a gentleman, were also two of the shareholders. It is quite likely that Rich gave, rather than sold, his sons their shares. Of the 12 other shareholders, one (Henry Collins) owned three shares, and two, William Samber and Thomas Scott (an executor of Rich's will), owned two shares each.[24] I count 20, but in BL Add Ch 9303, the number 19 is given. Five more shares were sold, presumably by Christopher, in the next two months.[25]

Just about everything seemed to be going well for Rich in early September. The theatre was very close to completion; the sale of shares was going well; clothes and scenes and properties were being accumulated; and a company of actors was being recruited. But Rich was doomed never to see the new theatre--his new theatre of which he must have been so proud--open. One day in September or October, in descending from his coach he injured his leg. The leg became infected, the infection spread, and soon Rich was moribund. On November 3, fully cognizant that his death was imminent, he drew up his will. On November 4 he died in his home in the passage that led to the Drury Lane theatre. A note at the beginning of (John) Rich's Register, volume I for 1714-23, kept by Christopher Mosyer Rich and now in the possession of the Folger Shakespeare Library in Washington, D.C., states the cause of Rich père's death "as a mortification, occasioned by a Hurt in his Leg, received as he was stepping out of a coach." Mortification in eighteenth century medicine--the term is still used today in certain areas of both Great Britain and the United States--meant gangrene or necrosis. At the time of his death Rich was within two months of his 67th birthday. Undoubtedly some members of the acting community attended the funeral; certainly the actors hired for the new season at Lincoln's Inn Fields would be there either out of courtesy to the deceased or deference to his sons. Probably his old friend Rupert Clarke was there, and Thomas Scott, one of the executors of his will. So were some, but probably not many of, the actors whom he had commanded from 1693 to 1709.[26] Perhaps some of the musicians and dancers and singers whom he had employed came. We can also presume that a not inconsiderable number said, "Good riddance" or its equivalent.

Christopher Rich was not buried until November 7, three days after his death. Since he was a resident of the parish of St. Clement Danes, although he declared himself in his will as being of the parish of St. Martin's in the Fields, his funeral service was held there.[27] Of the three bells that could be rung--the great bell at 8 shillings 8 pence, the small bell at 3s 6d, and the third bell at 5s 3d--it was the knell of the best bell that the mourners heard. Rich was not interred in the St. Clement Danes churchyard, so that its records don't tell us whether his sons had paid for a cloth shroud or a wool shroud, or the old ground instead of the new. He was "carry'd away" to the St. Andrews Holborn churchyard to be laid to rest in the family vault where, as his will states, his "Dear Wife was buryed." So were three of their daughters, Mary, Elizabeth, and Susan. Unfortunately none of these graves is visible today, all having given way to the Holborn Viaduct. The inscription on Rich's tomb has not come down to us, although it very well might have, had it come to the hand of John LeNeve, who compiled Monumenta Anglicana: Being Inscriptions on the Monuments of several Eminent Persons Deceased in or since the Year 1706 to the end of the Year 1715. He did list Rich as one of the "several Eminent Persons" included. Rich was described as "patentee of the Playhouse in Lincolns Inn Fields, died Nov. 3 or 4, 1714."

The will, made the day before he died, is very short and somewhat more pious than many other theatrical wills of the time that I have read.[28] He recognizes that he is "indisposed" in his health, "but of perfect mind and memory praised be Almighty God for the same. . . ." Before making his last will and testament Rich first resigns his "Soul to God the father of Spirits hoping for a joyfull resurrection both of body and Soul through the Meritts and passion of my Lord and Saviour Jesus Christ. . . ." Then he asks that all his just debts be paid. Next he states

111

I will and bequeath unto my Son John Rich and his heirs
three parts the whole in four even and equall parts to
be divided of all my Estate Right Title and Interest in
and to certaine Letters patent Granted by his late
Majesty King Charles the Second to Sir Wm Davenant . .
. and also three parts of all my Shares of Profitt
Cloathes Scenes &c ariseing out or by Virtue of the
Same and the other quarter part or Share of all my
Estate Right Title and Interest in or to the Said
Letters Patents and one Quarter part of all my Shares
of profitt Cloaths Scenes &c ariseing out or by Virtue
of the Said Letters patent I give and bequeath unto my
Son Xpher Mosyer Rich and his heirs. . . . .

The rest of his estate, both real and personal, Rich divided
equally between his two sons. The most important part of that
"rest" was in all probability a number of messuages in the Playhouse passage in Drury Lane and on Russell Street, just north of
Drury Lane theatre, and running more or less east-west between
Drury Lane and the Covent Garden market. There must have been at
least six of them, perhaps one or two more.[29] To be executors he
appointed his two sons as well as Rupert Clarke and Thomas Scott,
of the Custom-house, London, begging Clarke and Scott to aid and
assist his two sons in the execution of the will.[30]

Notes
Chapter Three: Frustration, Construction and Death:
Christopher Rich's Last Years (1709-1714)

[1]See his complaints to the Lord Chamberlain in December, 1710 or January, 1711 and to the Lord Chamberlain's secretary, Sir John Stanley in January, 1711 in Milhous and Hume, Coke's Theatrical Papers, pp. 167-69.

[2]See, for example, Shrewsbury's letter about financial problems at the Haymarket, probably in January, 1712, in Milhous and Hume, Coke's Theatrical Papers, p. 183.

[3]See his letter to Coke on November 20, 1713 and a claim filed probably in February, 1715 in Milhous and Hume, Coke's Theatrical Papers, pp. 206-07 and pp. 233-36.

[4]This probably occurred on March 15, 1715. See Milhous and Hume, Coke's Theatrical Papers, pp. 170-71.

[5]Look through pp. 207-23 and 231-36 in Milhous and Hume, Coke's Theatrical Papers.

[6]For a succinct account of the swiftly flowing chain of events between 1709 and 1714, see Barker, pp. 86-88.

[7]For details of Swiney's flight and the condition in which he left the Queen's, see Avery, Part 2, p. 292, who quotes from Colman's Opera Register.

[8]See Avery, Part 2, p. 301, who quotes from George Berkeley's letter to Sir John Percival as found in The Correspondence of George Berkeley and Sir John Percival (Cambridge, Mass., 1941), p. 115.

[9]Barker, p. 99, who cites the Masters' Reports, Vol. 335 (1716).

[10]s.v. "Lincoln's Inn Fields Theatre." The full title of the book is Theatrum Illustrata Graphic and Historic Memorials of Ancient Playhouses, Modern Theatres and other Places of Public Amusement in the Cities and Suburbs of London and Westminster. It was published in London by Robert Wilkinson.

[11]See PRO C11/2662/1 and C11/2732/81. In a letter to me dated January 6, 1985, Graham Barlow, of the Department of Drama of the University of Glasgow, a profound student of the theatrical architecture of the period, agrees with me "totally in regard to

the controversy over whether or not Shepherd built L.I.F. III. There is absolutely no evidence to support the suggestion." He goes on to suggest "that it was the work of Christopher perhaps with the aid of sons J. & C.M. and also a couple of bricklayers, one Boswell and the other Evans."

[12]See the Middlesex Land Register, 1712/6/11, in the Greater London Record Office.

[13]Middlesex Land Register, 1712/5/113.

[14]Middlesex Land Register, 1715/2/1.

[15]Middlesex Land Register, 1715/2/2.

[16]The index in the PRO in this case, KB 122/67 1713, as in other cases, gives only the few facts I have mentioned. Membrane 36, on which the case is detailed, is missing.

[17]See CP (Common Pleas) 40/3306 1714, Trinity, membrane 1846. Wise's administrator, Rebecca Wise, sued Christopher Rich, but since he had died, Rebecca sought an execution on John and Christopher M. Rich, who protested that they "have nothing."

[18]See KB 122/68, Hilary 1714, Middlesex, membrane 73.

[19]CP 40/3351 1722 Hilary, membrane 307.

[20]The amusing list includes some 49 separate items or groups of items.

[21]Thomas Lisle, who had built the first tennis court on the property, had made over half his estate to his son-in-law, Richard Reeve, probably in 1674 or 1675. About this time Reeve had invested Ŀ500 in repairs for the tennis court--then playhouse-- then tennis court again. Anne Reeve (née Tyler) was married to Richard, and Thomas was their son. According to Graham Barlow, Deodatus Champion obtained his moiety in the tennis court from Thomas Hiccocks, who had purchased it for Ŀ1725 in 1705 from Horatio Moore II, another son of Anne Reeve. For further information about the complicated backgrounds and inter-connections between the Moore, Lisle and Reeve families, see Barlow's unpublished Ph.D. thesis, From Tennis Court to Opera House, 1984.

[22]See Middlesex Land Register 1719/2/234.

[23]"Mr. Rich's Case on the bill for Restraining the Number of Playhouses, &c." It carries no date or place of publication, but it was probably printed around 1736 in London. I saw this three

sheet "case" at the Bodleian.

[24]The other nine shareholders were John Shaw of Eltham, Kent, son and heir of Sir John Shaw, Bart.; Charles Hale; John Eyles; Thomas Gilpin; Edward Periam; Daniel Outridge; Thomas Knight; John Heydon; and James Grascom(be). Each held one share. According to BL Add Ch 9305 Scott paid £240 to Christopher Rich and Rupert Clarke on Sept. 29, 1714.

[25]See Middlesex Land Register 1719/2/234.

[26]Fitzgerald, I, 388, citing no source, states that Rich's burial was "attended by several of those who had resisted his authority when living."

[27]See The Churchwarden's Account Books, St. Clement Danes, from 1707 to 1735, volume B15, in the Westminster Public Library, Buckingham Palace Road, London.

[28]See PROB. 11/543/228 in the PRO.

[29]See PRO C 38/448, which includes a schedule of tenants paying rent to John Evans, a bricklayer to whom the Riches owed money. In 1720 or 1721 tenants named Ogden, Smith, Edwards, Wilks & Company and Henry Rich are mentioned. In 1725 Chetwood, Palmer, Vaughan, Faulkner, as well as Smith and Wilks & Company, were paying rent.

[30]The will was probated on November 27 in the Prerogative Court of Canterbury.

CHAPTER FOUR

An Evaluation

The time has come for an evaluation of Christopher Rich, but
any evaluation of Rich must, in part, be a defense, because the
tendency among many theatre historians has been to accept Cibber's
judgments. And just as Pope has permanently damaged Cibber's own
reputation by the brilliant satire of The Dunciad, so has Cibber
permanently damaged Rich's reputation by the portrait he paints in
his Apology. Some of his dislike has rubbed off on his son Theophilus, who was 11 or 12 when Rich died and surely could not have
had any professional dealings with Rich. In his first Dissertation on Theatrical Subjects, published some 45 years after
Christopher's death, Theophilus termed him an "ignorant Tyrant,"
and a "cunning Shaver," and charged that he "was, perhaps, one of
the most dull, yet cunning Mortals that ever by Stupidity spoiled
a good Project--or, by Craft and Chicanery, got the better of
unguarded Men of superior Parts."[1] I cannot pretend that all the
other evidence--patchy and incomplete as it is--enables me to
assert that Rich was a man of probity, kindness, understanding,
foresight, and exemplary taste. Not at all. But surely we must
be constantly aware in reading Cibber's Apology that he is a far
from impartial witness: Wilks is not so bad as he is represented
in its pages, Owen Swiney not so good, Cibber himself not so equ-
ably tempered, reasonable and beneficent . . . and Rich not so
bad. When Cibber himself is not personally involved, he can be a
valuable and often fair judge, but we should not unhesitatingly
accept his dicta any more than his dates. On balance he is probably more often right than wrong, but it behooves us to recognize
misstatements, doubtful statements, and obviously biased statements. For example, Cibber attacks Rich for purchasing a share of
the patent not "to mend the Stage but to make Mony of it . . . ."
(Apology, p. 184) I find it hard to fault a man for that. How
many theatre managers who survived more than a very few seasons
had a different purpose? Note what Barker, a careful scholar and
an impartial judge, writes of Cibber: "He was interested in the
theatre, not in the drama: he was almost completely indifferent
to literary distinction."[1] When Cibber tells us that Rich had a
notion "that Singing, and Dancing, or any sort of Exotick Entertainments, would make an ordinary Company of Actors too hard, for
the best Set, who had only plain plays to subsist on," (Apology,
p. 180) we might well ask, "Was Rich not right?" Cibber asserts,

to say Truth, his Sense of everything to be shewn there [that
is, in the theatre], was much upon a Level, with the Taste of
the multitude, whose Mony weigh'd with him full as much, as
that of the best Judges. His Point was to please the

Majority, who, could more easily comprehend any thing they saw, than the daintiest things, that could be said to them. (Apology, p. 184)

Did not dozens of other managers do likewise? The ability to sense what the public wants is perhaps the most valuable of all qualities in a theatre manager. There can be no question, as I have pointed out already in my discussions of the various seasons, that the quality of new plays staged by Rich was at least on the level of those presented by his rivals. That Rich sensed plays alone could no longer continue to attract the multitudes is not to be charged as a fault. We have to remember that in his early days of management his company was vastly inferior to the set of splendid actors at Lincoln's Inn Fields. It is hardly to be wondered at that he resorted to singing, dancing, and other extra-dramatic attractions in order to draw patrons to his theatre. But he certainly was not the first (nor the last) to do so. All the elements of spectacle, dance and song had been introduced to the London stage years before Rich became a manager. Cibber himself acknowledges that it was Davenant who, faced with the finer acting of the King's Theatre company, "was forc'd to add Spectacle and Musick to Action; and to introduce a new Species of Plays, since call'd Dramatick Opera's . . . all set off with the most expensive Decorations of Scenes and Habits, with the best Voices and Dancers." (Apology, p. 57) The child acts, the animal acts, the acts featuring contortions of the body and voice, etc. were not innovations of Rich. It might well be maintained that Betterton and the other managers who vied with him for public approval should be more strongly condemned than he. Rich never went against his conscience in presenting any attraction. I am quite certain he would have denied that there was such a thing as a moral right and a moral wrong in scheduling entertainment at a theatre: what was right drew spectators; what was wrong created an empty house. But Betterton and Cibber and others were aware that their concept of the stage was being violated when they offered non-dramatic entertainment. Rich, it might be said, was amoral; Betterton and the others immoral. They knew they were doing the "wrong" thing and yet they did it anyway.

It is true he might very well have treated his performers better. Not infrequently the Drury Lane company under Rich found their salaries reduced, their benefits depleted. But, of course, this happened to other companies too. As has been shown, Rich did not introduce the idea of appropriating percentages of actors' benefit nights. But most other managers lowered salaries or restricted benefits only when impelled to do so by economic exigency. It is doubtful that Rich was similarly motivated.

Which brings us to another, perhaps the chief, charge that

117

may be laid against Rich: his chicanery vis-a-vis those men (and a few women) who invested in the theatres he managed, the so-called adventurers or shareholders. With them he seems to have demonstrated a kind of financial legerdemain. The number of suits against him is persuasive evidence that many of the shareholders believed they were being cheated, although Rich consistently reiterated that expenses devoured almost all the income. Through his skill as an attorney, and perhaps some innate deviousness, he was largely able to avoid making any considerable payments to these shareholders and equally to avoid legal responsibility. The profits he derived from Drury Lane and Dorset Garden were surely greater than he ever publicly acknowledged, although it is probable they were never so great as the various law suits alleged. Had Rich been as scrupulous in his accounting as he protested he was, he would have left very little to his sons. Had he been as successful as the plaintiffs in suits against him claimed, he would have left them much more.

While there were howls aplenty against Rich's management practices, so were there howls against every other manager. Review the history of the patent theatre before Rich assumed the direction of Drury Lane, and you will find all kinds of mismanagement, cupidity, deceit and dissimulation. Follow Hotson's tracing of the King's theatre at Drury Lane. Follow the problems of the United Company before Rich. Follow the history of almost any theatre manager and you will find a spate of negative criticism, sometimes justified, sometimes not. Let us consider for a moment Thomas Betterton, an outstanding actor and a theatre manager who in general seems to have enjoyed a favorable press. But the judgments about him were far from unanimous. Around the turn of the century Tom Brown and Robert Gould wrote harsh words about him and his co-managers at Lincoln's Inn Fields, and the author of A Comparison between the Two Stages termed him "a cunning old Fox."² But he and Mrs. Barry and Mrs. Bracegirdle, who together called the "Three Ruling B------s," were even more strongly condemned by one Frank Telltroth, obviously a pseudonym, in a preface to an unacted play, The Lunatick, published in 1705. Telltroth was writing under the impression that the new company at the Haymarket would not be under their control:

> There will . . . [be] no more Clandestine Sharing betwixt You without the rest; no more private Accounts, and Double Books; no more paying Debts half a score times over out of the Publick Stock, yet never paying them in reality at all. There will be no more sinking Three Hundred and fifty Pounds at a time in the Money repaid on a famous Singer's Account, but never accounted for to the rest of the Sharers; no more stopping all the Pay of the Under Actors on Subscription-Nights, when you were allow'd forty or fifty Pound a Night for the

House, besides the Benefit of the Galleries; no more sinking Court-Money into Your own Pockets, and letting the Sallary People and Under Sharers Starve without Pay; no more taking Benefit-Days in the best Season of the Year, and Dunning the Quality for Guinea-Tickets to help out the Defects of all the other above-named Perquisites; no fifty Shillings per Week for scowring Old Lace, nor burning it, and selling the Product for private Advantage; no Twenty Shillings a Day House-Rent; no sharing Profits with the Poetasters; nor Eating and Drinking out the other half before the Performance; no saving coals at Home, by Working, Eating and Drinking, &c. by the Stock-Fire; nor, in short, any Advantage to be made but by stated Sallaries, or the best Improvement of Natural Gifts, as far as Age, Ugliness and Gout will permit.[3]

It is clear that Telltroth is not always telling the truth, but undoubtedly some of the charges are accurate. Let me give another example, this time from the experience of a different manager, Owen Swiney, when he was directing the Haymarket. The wife of the recently deceased playwright George Farquhar was supposed to receive a free benefit night but Swiney insisted that she pay .80 35.[4] Note the strong emotional appeal here. I could cite other examples that would serve not to exonerate Rich but to implicate his rivals in the same kind of behavior. How much of an excuse is common practice? Summing up, we can say that the late 17th and early 18th century playhouse was not always a place of justice, peace, contentment, equality, of competent and fair management. Under Rich the theatre was probably as least as well off as it was under many other managers.

We have to balance out the good and the bad in the accounts of Rich. Cibber seems to impugn him for never being rash or hasty, (Apology, pp. 181, 213) yet he declares that Rich was "more a Slave to his Passions, than his Interest . . . ." (Apology, p. 110) Cibber insists that Rich could not distinguish between a good play and a bad, that he "knew no difference between Dryden and D'urfey. . . ." (Apology, p. 119) We might question this assertion, but even if it were true, we should note that Rich was astute enough to recognize his inadequacies and to hire Griffin, Powell, Wilks, and Cibber to assist him in the management. A man who knows he knows not is not so stupid. Rich was quick to recognize the value of advertising his programs, often in vivid detail, not only in the standard posted bills but, more innovatively, in newspapers. The more traditional Betterton seldom availed himself of this power of the press. A tabulation of Drury Lane's hits and misses will reveal that some of the biggest blunders in play acceptance and rejection were made by Cibber. Although Cibber regularly demeans Rich's intelligence, yet he states that Rich was aware that Powell was, au fond, a finer actor than Wilks, a judgment in which Cibber himself concurs. (Apology, p. 141) Pope quotes, with seeming approval, Rich's questioning an author who had submitted a play to him, "Pray do me the favor; Sir, to inform me; Is this your Tragedy or Comedy?"[5] This could, of course, mean that Rich could not differentiate between two such basic types, but I think it is clear that Rich's question shows that he was perceptive enough to recognize that the playwright had badly mixed the two genres. Addison (The Spectator, No. 5, March 6, 1711) relates Rich's turning down an opera design which featured Dick Whittington and his cat because it would have been necessary to introduce a great quantity of mice into the theatre and it was unlikely that the cat would be able to kill them all. No modern performers in the opera, Rich observed, could equal the Pied Piper. No great thought processes involved, certainly, but there is a measure of common sense which pervades almost all of Rich's theatrical activities except his architectural mania.

Christopher Rich hardly seems to have been an admirable man. Not infrequently he resorted to subterfuge, to tergiversation, to behavior that usually could be defended legally but not ethically. He could not measure up to those contemporaries of high principles. But he could measure up to many of his rivals in the very competitive profession of law; he could measure up to the average self-made man of his time. He was no philanthropist in the etymological sense of the word; no polymath; no lover of the drama as a sacrosanct art form; he was not immune to avarice. But he seems to have done a fair number of good deeds, whatever the motivation behind them. He was a father of whom his sons seem to have spoken no ill after his death. In a very protean time, he brought a measure of profitable management to the theatre. He was, in short, an average human being in many ways, gifted with a certain native shrewdness which was sharpened by training and experience in the law. His interest was business, and his business happened to be the theatre. Perhaps that sums it up best.

Notes
Chapter Four: An Evaluation

[1]See pp. 13, 14, and 16 for the quotations. The full title of Cibber's essay is Theophilus Cibber, to David Garrick, Esq; with Dissertations on Theatrical Subjects (London: 1759). The British Library copy is bound together with the second dissertation under the title Dissertations on Theatrical Subjects as they have several Times been delivered to the Public, (with general approbation) (London: 1756).

[2]Barker, p. 116.

[3]Milhous, Thomas Betterton, pp. 161-62, refers to Brown's "Amusements" and to Gould's "The Play-House." The quote from A Comparison is on p. 25. Even today there are conflicting judgments by well-qualified scholars about Betterton's managerial skills. As a manager he is termed "incompetent" by Shirley Strum Kenny in her article "Theatrical Warfare 1695-1710," Theatre Notebook, 27 (1973), 130-45, while Judith Milhous, Thomas Betterton, p. x, thinks that "the supposition that he was a 'bad' manager is peculiar and inaccurate."

[4]Milhous, Thomas Betterton, pp. 162-63, quotes this excerpt and comments on it. The Lunatick was published by B. Bragg in London. She recognizes there are some "obvious distortions" but acknowledges that the statements made by Telltroth add "to the weight of testimony against the senior actors."

[5]Milhous and Hume, Coke's Theatrical Papers, pp. 104-06, reprint the letter and comment on it.

[6]The Correspondence of Pope, I, 171. This is from a letter written to Henry Cromwell on August 29, 1709.

Bibliography

Allegations for Marriage Licenses issued by the Vicar-General of the Archbishop of Canterbury, July 1679 to June 1687. Ed. George J. Armytage. Harleian Society Publication 30. London: 1890.

Allegations for Marriage Licenses issued from the Faculty Office of the Archbishop of Canterbury at London, 1543 to 1689. Ed. George J. Armytage. Harleian Society Publication 24. London: 1886.

Avery, Emmett L., ed. The London Stage 1660-1800 Part 2: 1700-1729. Carbondale, Illinois: Southern Illinois University Press, 1960.

Baggs, Zachary. Advertisement Concerning the Poor Actors, who under Pretence of hard Usage from the Patentees, are about to desert their Services. London: July 8, 1709.

Barker, Richard H. Mr. Cibber of Drury Lane. 1939; rpt. New York: AMS Press, 1966.

Barlow, Graham. "Sir James Thornhill and the Theatre Royal, Drury Lane, 1705." The Eighteenth-Century English Stage. Ed. Kenneth Richards and Peter Thomson. London: Methuen, 1972.

Berkeley, George-Monck, ed. Literary Relics. London: 1789.

Brewster, Dorothy. Aaron Hill. New York: Columbia University Press, 1913.

Calendar of State Papers, Domestic Series 1694-1698.

Calendar of State Papers, Domestic Series 1694-1698.

Cibber, Colley. An Apology for the Life of Colley Cibber. Ed. B.R.S. Fone. Ann Arbor: The University of Michigan Press, 1968.

Cibber, Theophilus. Theophilus Cibber, to David Garrick, Esq; with Dissertations on Theatrical Subjects (London: 1759).

A Comparison Between the Two Stages. Ed. Staring B. Wells. Princeton: Princeton University Press, 1942.

Congreve, William. William Congreve: Letters & Documents. Ed.

122

John C. Hodges. New York: Harcourt, Brace, and World, 1964.

Cowper, Frances. A Prospect of Gary's Inn. London: Stevens & Sons, 1951.

Downes, John. Roscius Anglicanus. Ed. Montague Summers. London: n.d.

Dryden, John. The Letters of John Dryden. Ed. C.E. Ward. Durham, No. Carolina: 1942.

Fiske, Roger. English Theatre Music in the Eighteenth Century. London: Oxford University Press, 1973.

Fitzgerald, Percy. A New History of the English Stage. Vol. I. London: 1882.

Fletcher, Raymond J. The Pension Book of Gray's Inn. 2 vols. London: 1910.

Gildon, Charles. The Lives and Characters of the English Dramatick Poets. London: 1699.
The Post Boy Robb'd of his Mail. 2nd ed. London: 1706.

Highfill, Philip H., Kalman A. Burnim, Edward A. Langhans. A Biographical Dictionary of Actors, Actresses, Musicians, Dancers, Managers, and Other Stage Personnel in London, 1660-1800. 16 vols. in progress. Carbondale, Illinois: Southern Illinois University Press, 1973- .

Hotson, Leslie. The Commonwealth and Restoration Stage. 1928; rpt. New York: Russell & Russell, 1962.

Hume, Robert D. The Development of English Drama in the Late Seventeenth Century. Oxford: Clarendon Press, 1976.

_____, ed. The London Theatre World, 1660-1800. Carbondale, Illinois: Southern Illinois University Press, 1980.

Kenny, Shirley Strum. "Theatrical Warfare, 1695-1710." Theatre Notebook, 27 (1973), 130-145.

Kern, Ronald C. "Documents Relating to Company Management, 1705-1711." Theatre Notebook, 14 (Winter, 1959-1960), 60-65.

Langhans, Edward A. "The Vere Street and Lincoln's Inn Fields Theatres in Pictures." Educational Theatre Journal, 20 (1968), 171-185.

123

Loftis, John. Steele at Drury Lane. Berkeley, California: University of California Press, 1952.

Lowe, Robert W. Thomas Betterton. 1891; rpt. New York: AMS Press, 1972.

Middlesex Land Register. In Greater London Record Office, County Hall, S.E. 1.

Milhous, Judith. Thomas Betterton and the Management of Lincoln's Inn Fields, 1695-1708. Carbondale, Illinois: Southern Illinois University Press, 1979.

_____. "The Date and Import of the Financial Plan for a United Theatre Company in P.R.O. LC 7/3." Maske und Kothurn, 21 (1975), 38-76.

_____ and Robert D. Hume. "The Silencing of Drury Lane in 1709." Theatre Journal, 32 (1980), 427-447.

_____ and Robert D. Hume. Vice Chamberlain Coke's Theatrical Papers, 1706-1715. Carbondale, Illinois: Southern Illinois University Press, 1982.

Mr. Rich's Case on the Bill for Restraining the Number of Playhouses, &c. [London]: n.p., n.d. (in the Bodleian Library, Oxford)

Nicoll, Allardyce. A History of English Drama, 1660-1900. 4th ed. Cambridge: Cambridge University Press, 1952. Vol. I, II.

Novak, Maximillian E. "The Closing of Lincoln's Inn Fields Theatre in 1695." Restoration and 18th Century Theatre Research, 14, No. 1 (May, 1975), 51-52.

The Patentee. London: 1700.

The Players turn'd Academicks: or, A Description (In Merry Metre) Of their Translation From the Theatre in Little Lincoln's-Inn Fields, to the Tennis-Court in Oxford. London: 1703.

Pope, Alexander. The Correspondence of Alexander Pope. Ed. George Sherburn. Oxford: Oxford University Press, 1956. Vol. I.

Price, Curtis A. "The Critical Decade for English Music Drama, 1700-1710." Harvard Library Bulletin, 26 (1978), 38-76.

The Register of Admissions to Gray's Inn, 1521-1889, together with

The Register of Marriages in Gray's Inn Chapel, 1695-1754, by
Joseph Foster. London: Hansard Publishing Union, 1889.

The Registers of St. Stephen's Walbrook and of St. Benet Sherehog,
London. Ed. W. Bruce Bannerman and Major W. Bruce Bannerman.
Part I. Harleian Society Publication 49. London: 1919.

Rosenberg, Albert. "A New Move [Motive] for the Censorship of
Owen Swiney's 'The Quacks.'" Notes & Queries, 203 (1958),
393-96.

Sawyer, Paul. "The Date of John Rich's Birth." Theatre Notebook,
Jan.-March, 1954, p. 48.

_____. The New Theatre in Lincoln's Inn Fields. London: The
Society for Theatre Research, 1979.

Settle, Elkanah. The World in the Moon; an Opera, as it is
perform'd at the Theatre in Dorset Garden. 2nd ed. London:
1697.

Skipwith, Fulwar. A Brief Account of the Skipwiths of Newbold,
Metheringham, and Prestwould. Tunbridge Wells: 1867.

The Spectator

Summers, Montague. The Restoration Theatre. London: Kegan Paul,
Trench, Trubner, 1934.

Swiney (Macswiney), Owen. Grove's Dictionary of Music and Musicians. 1928 ed.

The Tatler

The Theatre Royal, Drury Lane and The Royal Opera House, Covent
Garden, Vol. XXXV of Survey of London, general ed. F.H.W.
Sheppard (London: The Athlone Press, University of London:
1970).

Theatrum Illustrata Graphic and Historic Memorials of Ancient
Playhouses, Modern Theatres and other Places of Public Amuse-
ment in the cities and Suburbs of London and Westminister.
London: Robert Wilkinson, 1825.

Three Original Letters to a Friend in the County, on the Cause and
Manner of the Late Riot at The Theatre-Royal in Drury-Lane.
London: 1763.

Van Lennep, William, ed. The London Stage 1660-1800 Part 1:

<u>1660-1700</u>. Carbondale, Illinois: Southern Illinois University Press, 1965.

Various primary materials in the British Library; Greater London Record Office, County Hall; Guildhall; Public Record Office; Westminster Public Library, Buckingham Palace Road (all in London); Eltham, Kent; Somerset Record Office, Taunton; Folger Shakespeare Library, Washington, D.C.; Huntington Library, San Marino, California.

128

Farquhar, George, 37, 119
  Beaux' Stratagem, The, 67
  Constant Couple, The; or,
    A Trip to the Jubilee,
    33, 34
  Inconstant, The, 38
  Recruiting Officer, The
  Sir Harry Wildair, 37
Fideli, Sigismondo, 32
Fiske, Roger, 49
Fletcher, John, 65
  Island Princess, The, 31
  Pilgrim, The, 34
  Rule a Wife and Have A Wife,
    50
Folger Shakespeare Library,
  110
Funeral, The, see Steele,
  Richard

Gibraltar; or, The Spanish
  Adventure, see Dennis, John
Gildon, Charles, 50, 68
  Measure for Measure (altered
    from Shakespeare), 35
Gilpin, Thomas, 115, n.24
Goodall, Mr., 84
Goodman's Fields Theatre, 106
Goring, Charles
  Irene, 73
Gould, Robert, 118
  Rival Sisters, The, 26
Granville, George, 65
  British Enchanters, The,
    56, 65
  She Gallants, The, 26
Grascombe, James, 115, n.24
Gravel Pitts field, 6, 7,
  106, 107
Gray's Inn, 2, 3, 4, 5, 6,
  10, 11
Gray's Inn Lane, 7, 107
Great Storm of 1703, 43, 44
Griffin, Philip, 25, 119
Grimaldi, Nicolini, 88
Grounds of Criticism in Poetry,
  see Dennis, John

Hale, Charles, 115, n.24
Hale, Henry, 74
Halifax, Lord, 28, 65
Hall, John, 44
Hampstead Heath, see Baker,
  Thomas
Handel, Georg Freidrich, 105
  Theseus, 104
Harris, Henry, 18, 26
Haym, Niccoli (Nicholini),
  56, 57, 105
Haymarket Theatre or Company,
  41, 45, 47, 48, 49, 54,
  55, 56, 58, 59, 60, 62,
  64, 65, 67, 69, 70, 71,
  72, 73, 75, 76, 81, 83,
  86, 88, 91, 104
Heidegger, J.J., 66, 71
Henry V, see Shakespeare,
  William
Heydon, John, 115, n.24
Hiccocks, Thomas, 114, n.21
Higgins (contortionist), 88
Hill, Aaron, 89, 90
Hill, Gilbert, 89
Hooke, Mary, 58
Hotson, Leslie, 7, 8, 118
Howard, Sir Robert, see
  Dryden, John,
  The Indian Queen
Hume, Robert D., 72, 84

Inconstant, The, see
  Farquhar, George
Indian Queen, The, see
  Dryden, John
Indulto, 81-82, 83
Iphigenia at Aulis, see
  Dennis, John
Irene, see Goring, Charles
Island Princess, The, see
  Motteux, Peter

130

132

Virgin Prophetess, The, see
  Settle, Elkanah
Virtuous Love, see Walker,
  William
Volpone, see Jonson, Ben

Walden, Frances, 8
Walker, William, 29, 30
  Virtuous Love, 30
Walsh, William, 55
Watson, John 40, 41
Watty, Edward, 74
Way of the World, The, see
  Congreve, William
Wilkins, Mrs. 34
Wilks, Robert, 35, 38, 53, 54,
  61, 62, 67, 76, 79, 80, 81,
  83, 91, 104, 105, 108, 109,
  116, 119
Williams, Joseph, 13
Wise, Hugh, 107
Wise, Rebecca, 114, n.17
Wonders in the Sun, see
  D´Urfey, Thomas
World in the Moon, The, see
  Settle, Elkanah
Wren, Sir Christopher, 6

Younger Brother, The, see
  Behn, Aphra